How to Draw a Circle

POETS ON POETRY

Derek Pollard, Series Editor
Donald Hall, Founding Editor

TITLES IN THE SERIES

ALSO AVAILABLE, BOOKS BY

For a complete list of titles, please see www.press.umich.edu

How to Draw a Circle

On Reading and Writing Poetry

DAN BEACHY-QUICK

University of Michigan Press
Ann Arbor

For questions or permissions, please contact um.press.perms@umich.edu

Published in the United States of America by the
University of Michigan Press
Manufactured in the United States of America
Printed on acid-free paper
First published July 2024

A CIP catalog record for this book is available from the British Library.

Library of Congress Cataloging-in-Publication data has been applied for.

ISBN 978-0-472-03970-8 (paper : alk. paper)
ISBN 978-0-472-22177-6 (e-book)

—for Kristy

. . . thy firmness makes my circle just,
and makes me end where I begun.

Contents

Acknowledgments

"The Hut of Poetry: Reading as Initiatory Experience," *Wonderful Investigations*. Milkweed Editions, 2012.

"Arcadian Survey," *The Arcadian Project Blog*. Editors: G. C. Waldrep and Joshua Corey.

"As in the Green Trees," Dan Beachy-Quick, 2015. "As in the Green Trees," *The Force of What's Possible: Writers on Accessibility & the Avant-Garde*. Editors: Joshua Marie Wilkinson, Lily Hoang. Nightboat Books, 2015.

"Of Time and Timelessness in the Poetic Sentence," *Taos Journal of International Poetry and Art*, 2014.

"To Arrive in Zeno's Thought: Reverie-on, Thinking-in, Peter Gizzi's 'A Panic That Can Still Come Upon Me,'" *In the Air: Essays on the Poetry of Peter Gizzi*. Editor: Anthony Caleshu. Wesleyan University Press, 2018.

"Poetic Geometries: *Moby-Dick* as Primer to Poetic Crisis," *Boston Review*, 2015.

"What Kind of Monster Am I?," *On Anne Carson*. Editor: Joshua Marie Wilkinson. University of Michigan Press, 2014.

"Ghosting the Line: Susan Howe and the Ethics of Haunting," *Quo Anima: Innovation and Spirituality in Contemporary Women's Poetry*. Editors: Jennifer Phelps and Elizabeth Robinson. University of Akron Press, 2018.

"Thinking as Burial Practice: Exhuming an Epistemology in Thoreau, Dickinson, and Emerson," *Wave Composition* (UK), 2015.

"'The Oracular Tree Acquiring': On Romanticism as Radical Practice," *Active Romanticism*. Editors: Julie Carr and Jeffrey Robinson. University of Alabama Press, 2015.

"Epistemic Flow," *Representations dans le monde anglophone 2017.2*, 2018.
"Lyric Consciousness," *Poetry Northwest*, 2018.
"Circularities: A Conversation," *MAP* (UK, online). Collaboration with
    Kylan Rice and Del Harrow.
"The Road Up Is the Road Down," *American Poetry Review*, 2024.

The Hut of Poetry

Reading as Initiatory Experience

The difficulty of being a nature poet is that nature always intervenes. The virtue of an honest ethic, to write only what one sees, to write only what one lives, becomes complicated by vision, becomes entangled by the experience of being in the world. Light travels over a course of time far more extensive than the miles it leaps across before it reaches our eyes. It takes thousands upon thousands of years for a photon to move through the labyrinth of the sun's dense center to the star's surface; it takes some eight minutes for light to speed from the star's surface to our eyes, where the objects it lands on enter our minds upside down, like bats sleeping in a cave. Light seems instant, but light is ancient; and if light is ancient, then so is the sight that light engenders. To write what one sees proves difficult because sight is a medium whose breadth encompasses time greater than the limits of human consciousness. To see is to open one's eyes to a source that includes oneself. Light comes with a history that includes our own. To see is to see double: the self as the self seeing, the world as the world seen. We do this seeing over the course of the years by which we count the extent of our lives. Years add up to something, but they do not add up to the world, they do not add up to the self in the world. Who am I when I say *I*? Not a container, not a vessel, filling over the course of a life with the evidence of having lived it. Not a silo slowly filling with grain. Not a sufficiency. Not a gathering resource unto myself. The difficulty with wanting to write about the world, the nature poet's truest creed, is that one finds there is nothing other than the world about which to write. The world is a limit—but a limit whose boundary is evanescent, the drama of the horizon line. Definition doesn't enclose when it does its truest work; it enacts, or reenacts, a process already occurred, a process that never stopped occurring. It began as we began: a single cell, a singular idea, definitive, commensurable, and then a force moves through it and it expands through the limit by which it had been known, by which it had known itself. It moves outward. It breaks itself so it cannot stay known.

When I think about writing poetry now, I think about an exhibit of ancient Southwestern pottery I went to see over a year ago. I remember one bowl in particular: brown earthenware, no glaze, at the bottom of which, in yellow slip, an ant-lion was painted. I thought the bowl contained a secret, that it lived a double life in the way poetry lives a double life. An object of use: the bowl was used to carry grain to feed the family of the man or woman who made it. An object of art, of mimicry: the bowl took its shape, almost comically because joyfully, from the sand bowl an ant-lion digs, waiting patiently at the bottom of the pit, for an ant to fall in and provide a meal. This bowl, in a sense, is a found form. The potter found her model in the ground at her feet, an aspect of attention all the more remarkable for the fact that the bowl is meant to carry food and the ant-lion's bowl-shaped trap serves the same purpose. Such work isn't imitation; it is realization through repetition, a form of conjuring, a form of charm, a "sympathetic magic" whose hope is that the manufactured object will share in the creative principle of the natural one. Many of the other vessels were broken at the bottom of the bowl, at the point where the burden of the grain, or the water, was greatest. Sometimes I imagine the work of writing as carrying that ant-lion bowl in my arms, and as I walk, the grain spills out the bottom onto the road I'm walking on, so that each step buries the seeds back into the earth from which they were pulled.

The other image that comes to mind when I think about poetry is a spiritual object of the Bamana people in Mali called a Boli. The Boli figure in the museum I frequently visited had a vaguely bovine shape: four legs, a thick body rising up into a hump, and the hump slanting forward, as if in the process—as of a cloud—of expanding slowly into a head that had yet to fully form. The Boli figure begins as a wooden block around which white cloth is wrapped. Then a mixture of mud, blood, and grain are packed in encrusting layers around the core, gradually building into the vaguely animal-like shape I stared at behind the glass case. The ambiguity of the shape keeps the object in almost constant refrain in my mind. The suggestion is of an animal that on closer scrutiny it could not be mistaken for—a work of representation in which recognition is triggered only to fail. The Boli seems to find a shape that allows it to exist in the world I live in, this world in which to see it is to think of it as bovine in structure, and another world in which such shapes come to no meaning, another world where every definite form dilates as clouds dilate when they extend and merge into the blue sky they had before obscured. The Boli's role in Bamana culture is to regulate the energy that moves from the universe to this world, as the atmosphere, and the clouds that fill it, regulates the sun's light. It is an object that keeps in balance a force, a spiritual energy that, unbalanced, could damage the world. Its likeness to a cow belongs to this world, this earth; its unlikeness to the cow belongs to the other world, the universe. It shares in both, and the oddity of its form is a result of the accuracy with which it performs its work. The Boli is a form that attends to its own formlessness. It shows the body at the point of pivot between two kinds of existence. It shows the cost of belonging to two worlds simultaneously but which in neither can it fully exist. It is the object as threshold, a door that is open only by being closed. It is a symbol. Its life is a symbolic life and brings those of us who believe in its power to our own symbolic nature.

The Boli could be seen as a poetic ideal; so could the ant-lion bowl be seen. They are of the world, of the environment, in the way poetry is of the world, of the environment. What unites all three concerns is their relationship to form. Poetry is an audacious experiment in form with form as the means of the experiment. Language, paradoxically enough, often obstructs the more fundamental work a poem attempts to do, filling the space of the poem with a worth that can be captured by the intelligence and removed. Such reading of poems for the value of what they may mean enforces a strict economy on poetry, a system of value that poetry itself is always trying to destabilize, to question if not destroy. But what is this work of poetry if it is not the work of making meaning through language? What can we find if we put our assumptions away, put our expectations away—if this is even a work that can be done—and turn to the poem for other reasons, other experiences? It helps, perhaps, to think of the poem not as content but cavern. It is not for us to ask *what is it?* It is for us to enter.

Reading is a method of entering; entering is a form of initiation. Form seen as such means that the poem functions on the page as a location that ceases to be a location. The poem on the page is no principality. It does not make a distinct place *in* the world, nor does it make a distinct place *of* the world. It is not a site to travel to, not a place of destination. Rather, the poem denies location because it acts—as the Boli figure acts—as a nexus between worlds, taking part in both worlds but belonging to neither, a threshold in which one must learn to dwell. The difficulty of reading poetry isn't the work of understanding what a poem may or may not mean. The truer difficulty is in learning to read so as to occupy the environment the poem opens, to suffer encounter with what is in the poem to encounter.

Our normal approach to reading, what we are taught to do in school, outlines a method whose end is a momentum that casts us out of the poem as the reward for having read it, our mind bejeweled with the profit of what we've found. To think of poetry as an environment, as a space of initiation, is to learn to read so as to lose a sense of meaning, to become bereft of what it is we thought we knew, to lose direction, to become bewildered. The first act of imagination in reading isn't the work of image-making but the work of entering the poem in which images exist, inexplicable ornaments within the form, each promising a knowledge to learn should one be patient enough to learn to see them. We enter the poem to threaten the security of the knowledge we possess before we read it. We enter the poem to be asked a question we will not ask ourselves otherwise, a question that begins at the point of our certainty. The fifteenth-century Indian poet Kabir knows the necessary difficulty of such work; he also knows the work's abundance:

Kabir says, seekers, listen:
Wherever you are
Is the entry point.[1]

When we enter as ourselves, we enter as seekers, as initiates. The work of reading as an initiate to poetry is seldom a work that feels like reading. It is not active but passive. It is learning to read so as to be read. Kabir again:

A tree stands without root,
without flowers bears fruit;

no leaf, no branch . . .
Dance done without feet,
tune played without hands,
praises sung without tongue,
singer without shape or form—
the true teacher reveals.[2]

Causality within this world the poem reveals is a faulty explanation of how tree, flower, dance, melody, and song come to be. The poem is the form the reader enters in order to see what the teacher reveals: that we dismiss the awful, inspiring fact of what exists when we attribute its existence to something other than itself. To the poetic initiate, the poem is the form one enters to hear the "praise sung without tongue," to hear the "singer without shape or form." Inside the poem the initiate finds the world "turned-around":

Turned-around Ganga dries up the ocean,
swallows the moon and the sun . . .
Turned-around rabbit swallows a lion . . .
Turned-around arrow strikes the hunter . . .
Turned-around earth pierces the sky.[3]

To describe the initiate's experience as paradoxical misnames its more startling force. Within the poem each object becomes retranslated into its actual nature—each object becomes "turned-around." To be "turned-around" isn't simply to appropriate the attributes of a contradicting object—river drying up ocean instead of feeding it, rabbit devouring lion, arrow hunting the hunter, earth stabbing sky. Kabir uses paradox paradox-ically, contradiction contradictorily, to reveal, as a "true teacher" must, that the distance between subject and object is unsteady, is susceptible— within the world within the poem—of profound reversal. To read is also this work of being turned-around.

The turned-around poem reads the reader. Reading is a work done to us before it is a work we do. The turned-around reader is the book's book.

But to better see what poetry as an initiatory environment might mean, we should look at examples of what such spaces are, of how they function, and what our own work of reading might be in such a context. Mircea Eliade, in *Rites and Symbols of Initiation*, outlines the nature of initiatory experience:

> The term initiation in the most general sense denotes a body of rites and oral teachings whose purpose is to produce a decisive alteration in . . . the person to be initiated. In philosophical terms, initiation is equivalent to a basic change in existential condition; the novice emerges from his ordeal endowed with a totally different being from that which he possessed before his initiation; he has become *another*. . . . Initiation introduces the candidate into the human community and into the world of spiritual and cultural values.[4]

The "ordeal" of initiation occurs, as does a poem on a page, in a location that is not a place. A "sacred ground" is prepared, and on that ground, or near it, an enclosure is built. The preparation of the ground returns it to a Chaos on which the enclosure as Cosmos is built. The enclosure often represents the body of a divinity, and to enter it is to enter the body, to walk in through the mouth, to be devoured. Initiation requires death, to encounter death. In some cultures, initiates return from the sacred ground to their mothers, who can no longer see them, mothers who wail in mourning at the death of their sons as their sons walk among their mothers. Some initiates return with a new name and no memory of their previous life. Others rituals are even more startling:

> On a particular day the novices, led by a priest, proceed to the Nanda [a stone enclosure, often hundreds of feet long, a great distance from the village] in single file, with a club in one hand and a lance in the other. The old men await them in front of the walls, singing. The novices drop their weapons at the old man's feet, as symbols of gifts, and then withdraw to the cabins. On the fifth day, again led by the priests, they once more proceed to the sacred enclosure, but this time the old men are not awaiting them by the walls. They are then taken into the Nanda. There "lie a row of dead men, covered with blood, their bodies apparently cut open and their entrails protruding." The priest-guide walks over the corpses and the terrified novices follow him to the other end of the enclosure, where the chief priest awaits them. "Suddenly he blurts out a great yell, whereupon

the dead men start to their feet, and run down to the river to cleanse themselves from the blood and filth with which they are besmeared."[5]

The link between such ancient initiatory ordeals and the work of reading poetry seems spurious unless it feels intuitive. A blank page is one version of chaos, and the lines built on that ground form a dwelling. It is a strange dwelling, meaningless before entered—a confusion of black marks on a white page. By reading it we enter it. Entering it we find a world inside it. Inside it we can see. We find ourselves in a world that does not exist by any normal measure of existence, a world we see within our minds that we enter only by attending to something outside of ourselves. The movement outward and the movement inward are simultaneous. When we read, we hear the old ones singing. To learn to sing ourselves—that secret our initiation introduces us to—is to find ourselves walking upon the corpses of those who sang before us, pulling from their mouths the words we find in our own, giving to those words our own breath. When we learn to sing, the dead leap up and wash the grime from their bodies. Tradition promises us this resuscitating work.

Such a vision of the poem realizes Dickinson's own aspiration for art as a house that "tries to be haunted." Dickinson, like Kabir (poets of deep congruence), provides help in other ways. Dickinson understands not only that the poem is a form that waits to be haunted, but she also gives her readers a glimpse into what the effect of that haunting, what the poem as an introduction to death, might be:

I felt a Funeral, in my Brain,
And Mourners to and fro
Kept treading—treading—till
it seemed
That Sense was breaking through -
And when they all were seated,
A Service, like a Drum—
Kept beating—beating—till
I thought
My Mind was going numb -

And then I heard them

lift a Box
And creak across my [Brain crossed out]
Soul
With those same Boots of
Lead, again,
Then Space—began to Toll,

As all the Heavens were
a Bell,
And Being, but an Ear,
And I, and Silence some
strange Race
Wrecked, solitary, here -

And then a Plank in
Reason, broke,
And I dropped down, and
down—
And hit a World, at every
+plunge,
And +Finished knowing—then -[6]

"I felt a Funeral, in my Brain" offers readers a lesson in poetry as initiatory experience. The poem's first line introduces us to death, but a death that occurs in the mind before it occurs in the body. The poem is that strange space we can enter only mentally, as the page refuses the materiality of the body's trespass. We must leave—to a curious degree—our body behind when we read. The rites of the mourners, those unnamed people whose "Boots of Lead," with their heavy step, strike "Space" into tolling. That ringing bell marks death; it rings across the universe. The casket—like the Boli figure—mediates, in Dickinson's poem, two worlds. One is the world where sense is but common sense. The other world is where Being is "but an Ear" and the "Heavens were a Bell." Kabir's thought that the "singer has no shape or form" comes to astounding realization. For Heaven's Bell isn't a bell, and the knowledge its ringing brings—a knowledge not factual in nature but, rather, a resonating drone that vibrates within the Being of Dickinson's Ear—results in the plummet that actual knowing is. Knowledge isn't Reason but the Plank that in Reason breaks. Song, too, sings via vibration. Every line of a poem is a Plank in Reason. To "Finish knowing" is to break through the floor Reason has built. Kabir and Dickinson know that the hut of poetry has no floor.

Dickinson's definition of how she knows when she's read a poem comes into a new light: "If I read a book [and] it makes my whole body so cold no fire can ever warm me I know *that* is poetry. If I feel physically as if the top of my head were taken off, I know *that* is poetry."[7] The poem isn't funereal in its relation to death. The funeral occurs in the brain. As one vision of knowledge is plunging downward through Reason, so a parallel vision of knowledge is the loss of the top of one's head. The image isn't meant to depict a decapitation. Rather, it depicts the removal of that other plank, the skull's top, whose plank is the basement of the universe. That plank removed opens the mind to the whole. It is a death that precedes life. To read is the most common form of encounter with the dead. The dead on the blank page need not remain dead. Time in the page is different from time in the world. The page is that impossible cavern in which no echo has ever ceased echoing, in which no word has ever died, though the mouths that sang them have been lost in the earth centuries ago. Death in the poem is only a pause before rebirth. Death is but a delay inside the form.

Language offers a method of experiencing death without dying. Language in a poem builds a form on a blank page and, by building that form, brings into use the strange, chaotic power the blank page represents—the power of the unseen, unspoken, unsung world that could be seen, spoken, and sung. The poem on the blank page houses a creative center infinitely larger than itself, than its own lined confines, but a power that has no useful ends without suffering the impossible limit of the poem's form. The forging of limit through form is the poem's most fundamental work, and the result of that work is that the poem becomes not a vessel of knowledge conveyed but a dwelling where knowledge occurs. What we find inside the poem—for those of us who learn to read so as to enter—is the language by which the poem is built. We find words and the world those words evoke. Words, as does the Boli figure, live a double life. The semiotic crisis of modern poetics, the sense of a word's arbitrary connection to the object it names, the indefinite distance between signifier and signified that feels as if it threatens language's ability to name anything at all, is not a modern crisis. Language is the ancient crisis that introduces us, over and over again, to the necessary failure that words in relation to the world bear. It is not necessarily a semiotic difficulty so much as it is a mimetic one. We tend to see poems as vehicles of semiotic information when the poem becomes nothing more to us than ink on a page, the flat plane of the second dimension.

When the poem becomes for us not a page but a structure, when it is a place of entry and so of initiation, when we are the initiates inside it, language's double life becomes of profound use. Regardless of the arbitrary relation of a name to the named, the work occurring within that relation, the work words teach us to do, functions just the same. We read and recognize the world to which the words refer. Words function magically in the poetic environment, in the hut of the poem. That words give to the world a set of names by which we remember, we know it is an accidental quality of the deeper work words do. That deeper work is a magical work. That words give to the world a set of names by which we remember it, by which we know it, is an accidental quality of the deeper work words do. The words out of which the poem is built always attempts to enact the world they name, to share in the nameless fact of the world's actuality by repeating it, by replicating it, in the words by which it is known. Within the poem we find a world in addition to the world. We return to those poems that matter most to us not because we have something else to learn but because the world of that poem has become for us our home.

But a home is never the world—a home is a separation from the world. A poem is never the world—a poem is a separation from the world. The world we read and in reading see never stays a world. Language's gift to us is its failure. The enchantment of language is superseded in importance by its disenchantment. The pivot between those two extremes mimics death. We are given a world that we lose. A poem's formal life is filled with totems that deny the death the poem's larger work forces us toward. Lines evoke the process of ritual, an attention always broken before it's complete, where enjambment demands that the attention find a way to renew itself, to resurrect the image the blank margin has just destroyed.

Literary tropes mimic a magic that recognizes death and, in doing so, gives us the means to undo it. Rhyme, properly heard, refuses to let sound die but recognizes that it cannot call back the object it records in its original state. Rhyme calls forward the same sound in new form, as if the deeper meaning of a word had little to do with its lexical content and everything to do with the syllable chanting inside the definition. The body is different but the breath is the same. A poem initiates us into death so as to awaken us into life, into this world that requires new eyes to see. What unites initiatory experience throughout cultures is the necessity of dying so as to leave behind one mode of interacting with the world and enter into another one. One sense of what poetry offers us is precisely this initiation into death so as to emerge from the poem more alive. We ask art to give us new eyes—to do so we must learn to put our old eyes out. Light is ancient, and the mistake we most often make is in thinking that to see is an instantaneous work. When we see with new eyes, we see anciently. Poetry offers us the initiation into such light and, through such light, a life that sees the world in the continuous present. We put time away when we walk out of the poem and into the world. When time catches up, when we become again all too mortal, we return to the poem in order to remember how to return to the world.

When we read as initiates, and when the space of the poem is the space of initiation, we undergo the ancient ritual of deserving to live in the world in which we're alive. We put "childish things away." That state in which the world dangles like a bauble on the string of the mobile the baby reaches her hand toward is replaced by entering into the world with the overwhelming sense of life's sacredness. Initiation is the introduction to the fragility of the world by which it is seen as most whole and holy. We see that fragility by recognizing our own—a realization that must step through mortality in order to step past it. To read a poem in this sense is to commit a necessary suicide. No, that's the wrong sentiment, the wrong word. One might say instead that to read the poem is also—secretly, anciently—to prepare oneself sacrificially, to make of one's mind and one's heart that peculiar offering that lends life to the page being considered. In such a notion we hear Whitman's song:

The smallest sprout shows there really is no death
And if ever there was it led forward life, and does not wait at the end to arrest it,
And ceas'd the moment life appear'd.

All goes onward and outward, nothing collapses,
And to die is different from what any one supposed, and luckier.[8]

Poetry initiates us into the possibility of just such a supposition, anathema as it is to any common common sense. One ceases to be an initiate when the world is real to you. Poetry is difficult because it returns us to reality. To get there we enter the world the poem opens within itself. We suffer the dizzying repetitions, the marvelous representations. We become the poets we read, come into this sense of ourselves only through the loss of the same. We are with Apollo in Keats's "Hyperion," waking to his own power:

> —Thus the God,
> While his enkindled eyes, with level glance
> Beneath his white soft temples, steadfast kept
> Trembling with light upon Mnemosyne.
> Soon wild commotions shook him, and made flush
> All the immortal fairness of his limbs—
> Most like the struggle at the gate of death;
> Or liker still to one who should take leave
> Of pale immortal death, and with a pang
> As hot as death's is chill, with fierce convulse
> Die into life[9]

Life, world: we die into it. Words kill us. We lose the tops of our heads. Then we open our eyes. Then we walk out of the poem into the world.

Arcadian Survey

It looks out and it looks backward, back through its own looking, the pastoral eye. This vision, teleological and etiological at once, reaching toward limits it wants to resist, reaching down toward roots it wants to pull up, marks for me the basic motions of the pastoral art as I've found myself practicing it—mostly unintentionally, finding myself caught in the tow of imagination's own necessity—over the past many years. But rather than investigate the pastoral so as to make a claim, part phenomenological and part aesthetic, rather than risk articulating it, cutting it into its component parts only to hope it can be stitched back together again, I'd like merely to do what feels most caring—as I also see the pastoral as a primary mode of poetic care—to take a survey, so to speak, to walk along the edges of my thinking, these pastoral edges, and describe some of what I see.

1. The Soul Seeks an Erotic Ground

I've come to take very seriously the somewhat absurd rendition Socrates offers Phaedrus when, retracting his earlier speech praising the non-lover over the lover, he tells him of the nature of the soul. The soul, he says, is tripartite. Socrates offers a metaphor. It is like a charioteer driving two horses, one of noble breed and fluent in the driver's commands, and one bad, always struggling to resist the directions imparted to him. In this vision the soul is winged, and the chariot flies through the heavens where the Forms exist, following the path of the god whose nature this soul most partakes of: a poet might be of Apollo's train, but so many souls are flying about—some in astonishing order, flying in harmony, and others in astonishing disarray, careening into others and knocking off their wings.

It is this unwinged soul, such a soul's descent, that feels of most interest to me. Such a soul is hard to control, as the willful horse pulls against the driver's wish for order, the wish to return to ideal truth. The dark horse pulls downward toward a ground that does not yet exist, a ground that begins to form—so I imagine it—when the soul, through the senses of this dark horse, comes across someone he finds beautiful. At the sight of this person's beauty, the dark horse pulls so hard the charioteer must draw back on the reins with such strength that the bit bloodies the mouth, so hard he pulls both horses over. But the dark horse is relentless, forcing the others to near what he finds so irresistible, so near that the other parts of the soul also see this beauty; they see how in it there is some vestige of what in those pure heights they once saw, and the driver pulls back less hard on the reins, and the soul nears what fascinates it.

In some sense, this nearing beauty, the tension that is simultaneously erotic and epistemological, of sense and of soul, creates the very ground upon which this approach can occur. It is a ground riddled with fault. In fault it finds splendor. This ground, this field, this sudden acre, it forms between two opposed realities, between the Ideal and the Actual. I might say the flowers reach up toward the world that is denied by the world toward which the roots reach down. Far more than the object of beauty itself, I think of the pastoral as providing the ground upon which the difficulty of beauty can be encountered, can be suffered, for beauty seems to confound within itself the very contradictions that mark this meadow on which we find ourselves uneasily landed, this meadow, as Robert Duncan describes the same, "that is a made place," where "the shadows that are forms fall."[1] Here is where the shadows gain substance and breathe, in their beauty breathe, a place more than real and less than real, this rootless ground in which the mind takes root, hovering there in nothing, between truth and reality, belonging to neither for being claimed by both.

II. Poussin, *Et in Arcadia Ego*

Three men and a woman wander through Arcadia, all shepherds, and find on a rise a large gravestone, its face weathered by age. One shepherd leans on the stone looking down as his friend runs his finger along the words etched into the stone. He touches those letters as if tracing their shape reveals nothing of their sense, and there is the first sign

Arcadia introduces me to, a kind of pun or stranger, a kind of "un," in which what words there are are forms of absence that mark absence, that mark absence as present, as the letter is formed by the absence of stone. The third man looks down and, watching his friend touch the incoherent letters, looks back and up at the woman, finger pointing at the stone but not touching it, as if asking her to look and explain it, as if she has the ability to do what none of the others do, that she knows how to read the signs. But she won't look. She looks down at the ground, a look of old called *aidos*, a look of shamefastness marked by the lowering of the lid over the eye, as if what is known is not to be known, as if one should know and also not know what one knows, and so she looks down, looks down, as is she sees in the ground some hole, not the open grave but, worse, a hole in the ground that is a hole in the canvas, a hole that doesn't simply break the ground but pierces it open to nothingness. Or is it just slightly different? She looks down and sees the edge, the very edge where Arcadia ends.

But perhaps her sense of shame offers us another instruction. Maybe it's more than this warning that even in Arcadia death exists, that even here death says "I am." Arcadia asks us to doubt something hard to doubt, to dismantle something we assume isn't merely a construct: self, the self-same, this one I mean when I say "I." In ancient Greece, "I" was a word found on gravestones. The linguist Daniel Heller-Roazen writes:

> The first person of the memorial object, from this perspective, appears as a purely written phenomenon. It constitutes the sign not of a living being but of its absence, and only as such can it mark the decease of the one it commemorates. Svenbro recalled, in this context, the etymological account of the first-person pronoun once proposed by Karl Brugmann, according to which the Greek *ego*, as well as its Indo-European relations, derives from a neuter noun, meaning simply, "hereness": originally, "I" would signify the insubstantial being of whatever can be indicated as "here," be it animate or inanimate, human or inhuman, its expression spoken or written.[2]

Here I lie. I don't mean me. It meant a word that spoke of me, and not as a person, not as an identity, but as a location. I locate myself at this very point that in death is a point of absence. If Poussin's painting does mark Arcadia's edge, then it must mark the point at which it begins, not simply where it ends. And perhaps our entrance into Arcadia requires of us a certain burial, a burial of what in me says "I," the self-same me where who I am is reducible to the experience of my life, to what I feel and what I think, but what I feel and what I think were just the ways in which the world etched onto me a damage that allows me to say "I." What happens when we bury that damage and walk into the field? What if I no longer can say I hurt in just this way but bury the whole harm and walk away? Do I multiply? Do I find that who I am are three men and a woman, all shepherds? That the image of my soul is quaternary? Not a charioteer and two horses but those very figures in *Et in Arcadia Ego*, all four of them, three who cannot read and a fourth who will not look at the letters because, perhaps, she still can.

III. An Eternal Pasture Folded in All Thought

What can a field teach us about desire? Keats suggests we put away the ease of that erotic primer, the "birds and the bees," and reconfigure how it is we imagine our imagination:

> It has been an old Comparison for our urging on—the Bee Hive—however, it seems to me that we should rather be the flower than the Bee, for it is a false notion that more is gained by receiving than giving. No, the receiver and the giver are equal in their benefits. The flower, I doubt not, receives a fair guerdon from the Bee. Its leaves blush deeper in the next spring, and who shall say between Man and Woman which is the most delighted? Now it is more noble to sit like Jove than to fly like Mercury. Let us not therefore go hurrying about and collecting honey-bee like, buzzing here and there impatiently from a knowledge of what is to be arrived at; but let us open our leaves like a flower and be passive and receptive, budding patiently under the eye of Apollo and taking hints from every noble insect that favors us with a visit.[3]

Imagination here alters, here in Arcadia. It is no longer that construction that takes what *is* and, in some dissatisfaction, plumes the mind with what isn't. Like the eye that open receives what enters it, this Arcadian imagination is likewise open, radical most in its passivity, its "diligent indolence," a quality erotic in that it depends upon another to complete itself, a quality creative because the whole field depends upon each flower, each eye or each mind, not a plan or a system, something even less than, and so better than, hope, to remain open, budding into patience.

It is into such a meadow I imagine Robert Duncan returning to when he is permitted. To be "permitted" implies some permission has been asked or something has been offered, a simple rite of initiation, some gift, or some sacrifice. Ask the shepherds before the grave what I must offer, and in the asking itself, I cease to be anything more than a "hereness," not a wanderer through a field but a field that through another field wanders. That ground, as Duncan gives it to us, is one of subtle paradox, one in which the relationship between the given and the made finds itself reversed, and the made-thing is the given, the preexisting, the eternal. The mind, the flower-like mind, is given the scene it also makes up: "that is not mine, but is a made place // that is mine, it is so near to the heart." Curious how the mind, dislodged from the seat of its reason, offers to the heart the field it finds folded within thought—and nearing the heart, that field, that made-place, becomes mine. The mind here seems circulatory, of the blood, and thought seems a kind of spirit or pneuma in the oldest sense: breeze-like bearing on it what it may chance to carry, all the made-things given to the mind when the mind is something other than merely "mine."

In the field the poet is a *techne*, a maker, and the poem is *poema*, the made-thing. I am a location called here, anonymous, one and many, as is the ancient chorus. That word, too, is of this ground, moving back through its etymology past the dancing singers it names to the ground on which the singing dance occurs. Tracing that motion gives to my mind the made-thing of pastoral thought, not the song but the ground on which the song occurs, and the foot there that dances, and the voice there that sings, is mine and not-mine, is one and many.

IV. Interlude

ARCADIAN

I could not stop my hands clapping. I clapped
And clapped. I clapped as in the dirt the bird collapsed,
As worms grew wings, I clapped.

A man stood in a river balancing
A grape on his lips. His tears fell in the current
Swept them away. He kept performing

His trick: grape hovering over the hole
Of his open mouth and never dropping in.
I clapped and I could not stop

My hands from wanting to cover my mouth
But they would not. They clapped
And I listened to them clap—a noise

That if there were woods would echo in
The woods. But there were no woods
I could see. Only a man. Twigs in his hair.

Bent over the water where the water stood
Most still. A tree fell in the woods—
He kept speaking to his own face—

Is true if and only if a tree fell in the
Woods is true if and only if—
He kept speaking to his face in the water

As I clapped, applauding the logic
That needed no belief. Like the shadows
Of bird's wings, the shadows of my hands

On the ground. If there were birds
I could believe in
the birds so I let myself look up.

One bird kept exploding in the sky.
One flower kept dying. Isn't it happy? a child asked,
Everything eating the sun? Isn't it

Happy? Isn't it—she asked, laying down
On her back in the grass—happy?
Everything eating the sun? Isn't it—

V. The Apple in the Tree

Anne Carson notes that "in a certain usage in Homer, . . . epic diction has the same verb (*mnaomai*) for 'to be mindful, to have in mind, to direct someone's attention to' and 'to woo, court, be a suitor.'" Not knowing ancient Greek myself, I cannot say with any genuine knowledge that the same verb is at work in lyric poetry nor the version of lyric that unfolds in the pastoral. But I can say with necessary uncertainty that it feels true to me: that in this meadow we've entered, in Arcadia, to think and to desire are one and the same thing, and we find the grass weaves together as a bound that "holds against chaos." It may be that the grass is rooted in that chaos it resists, not a fact exactly but a poetic logic that understands the work of imagination unfurls for us the leaves of an erotic epistemology.

Walk long enough in Arcadia and you'll find this tree. Sappho describes it:

as the sweetapple reddens on a high branch
*   high on the highest branch and the applepickers forgot—*
no, not forgot: were unable to reach[4]

The pastoral mind has, I suspect, a curious relation to the beauty of the unattainable, the desire of thinking's reach. It undoes the ground back to chaos and then rewrites it; and in the reformed field, should one be permitted to enter, the apple is at hand, the sweetapple on the highest branch, not because the tree has been cut down or the branches climbed but because the ground itself is nearer the object of the heart's thought and the mind's desire.

As in the Green Trees

I want to be at work.

The most profound gift I know is the gift of being at work: that habitual effort to attend to the world in all its daily facts, in all its daily facts even as the facts themselves begin to dismantle the edifice of their own construction, even as the world verges from the known thing to the thing resistant to all knowing. I want to be at work, at work in it, in the world—and my work happens to be a work in words, and to be at work in words day-to-day, fact-to-fact, face-to-face, well, such is the happiness of the soul, my soul's happiness.

What makes me happy? The things I worry most about. The worry of the way in which the real is real, the actual *sincerely* actual, not just the thingness of the thing, not just *haecceity* but also the reality of the less than real and the more than real: imagination, thought, love. Is this embarrassing to admit? That I think a poem must find in itself a way to be involved with the reality of love, love's thinking, and thinking's love. Well, I do.

Every form of pre-assumed exclusion worries me, be it the avant-garde's ever-forward march from the status quo, be it an encouragement toward nothingness in the face of an ever-appropriating empire. I like to think a poem alters what power swallows it; I like to think a poem alters the sterile current state of affairs into a realm of first thought and first vision. A poem *altars*. But I am one who also thinks "the sun is a morning star," and that blank-page dawn-light wakes me to the work that wakes me to the world that wakes me to the curious fact that I spend my days darkening some form of light with words, with words, with words that are some form of world. Sorry. I see I'm caught again in love's riddle.

. . .

I had a dove and the sweet dove died,
And I thought it had died of grieving;
O, what could it grieve for? Its feet were tied
With a silken thread of my own hand's weaving:
Sweet little red feet! Why would you die?
Why would you leave me, sweet bird, why?
You liv'd alone on the forest tree,
Why, pretty thing, could you not live with me?
I kiss'd you oft, and gave you white pease;
Why not live sweetly as in the green trees?[1]

. . .

The poet discovers that she is in a bind; it cannot be helped. The bind is that the poem is binding. We tie a silken thread around the feet of what we love, a black silken thread, just a line. What is wild we sing into presence, and then wildness worries itself, worries itself, almost to death. Is it too much to say that a poem may spend its life tying together a dove's feet only to wish most devoutly that the dove would sing as if never bound? Too much to suggest that devout wish can only come about by the work of tying a silken thread around those "little red feet"? Can it be true, this riddle, phenomenal and formal and strangely categorical, that we can only wish the work undone by doing first the work? How is it that cause follows consequence? Poet, how? How is it the poem written means only the next poem must be begun? What? What is it you hear? Oh, that again? The dove singing in the morning star's blank light.

. . .

To be honest, I no longer know what experimental poetry is. To be more honest, I no longer care. A rhyme is a conceptual thing, just as a "tear is an intellectual thing."[2] A poem's formal life is my primary concern, never the same twice.

"Twice." That very word is like a bell to toll me back to my doubled self! Voice with other voices filled. It echoes anonymously. The chorus wonders how to step in from the margin. All that dancing at the edges, all that delay, all that witness in hesitation. Slow down the moment and still it seems—as it always has—mostly eternal.

I think I've found that poetry confounds. I mean this sentence in the oldest, most riddling sense. To divide a field in two, to name one half tradition and one half experiment, undoes the confounding realm where poetry innately occurs—the *chorus*, the lyric threshing ground, where the chaffy grain is winnowed, where the doves glean when the gleaners leave. I want both; I want the field entire. I want the lyric poem to be that place, that sacred space, devoted to tradition as radical experiment. There a trope such as rhyme doesn't just please the ear but keeps current that old symbolic cycle, where time does not proceed infinitely in either direction—forever's past and forever's future—but locates itself in the continual repetition of one ongoing *is*, the past always a form of prophecy. At the same time, in the same poem, I see how a line refutes the symbolic, how words gather to themselves the cunning tricks of simultaneity, of polysemy, of puns. But who cares what I want? Not even I do.

Can a poem know and also not know what it knows?

Another riddle to which I don't know the answer. Sometimes I feel a poem knows its ignorance; sometimes I think a poem ignores its knowledge. I can't plan on confusion, can't find a system to make confusion real. Nor can I do the same with clarity. I can just write a line that might become two, two that might become four, and so on, maybe eternally, until I realize I'm lost, the page's leaf has become the forest's tree; I'm lost in the green trees, my hands filled with silken threads, wondering how it is that one lassos song, wondering if song knows that way out, wondering if song ignores what it knows and wants those who find themselves lost only to become, to become more lost.

Of Time and Timelessness in the Poetic Sentence

I want to examine as simply as I can differences, real or imagined, between a sentence and a line of verse. Of course, one of the implicit complications in such work is that the imaginary, in poetic realms, has a claim *in* or *as* reality. Such is the danger of the questions that must be asked: that they sever one form of linguistic life from another and create a hierarchy of values instead of the deeper goal, an appreciation of the complex whole that undermines our ability to make such judgments. I want what I suspect most of us here want—to be thrilled by those interpenetrations at which the word "poetic" hints, seeking some admittance into that penetralia at the very heart of language's whole architecture, where the numen behind her sibylline veils speaks. I want to know how to pay attention and to trust, because I must, that attention is itself the prerequisite for poetic apprehension. *Apprehension* feels like a key word: grasp, fear, understanding. It speaks of that extraordinarily unstable terrain between the physical sensation of the world and the reality of the mind that absorbs it, keeping in delicate, imperfect balance, realms of experience that can never wholly coexist—the actual and the ideal. And so we find ourselves continually reinitiated into that curious agony that consciousness cannot help but be: that both world and thought are real, and as much as a stone is syllable of the actual, so is a word a kind of stone.

1. The Sentence

Sentences are made of words. Those words behave according to certain laws, none of them immutable. The sentence seems, at some level, to be the expression of those laws: grammar's undergirding beneficence.

Most often we move from subject to verb to object. But it grows complicated.

Oddities in syntax awaken our sympathies. We gain some context for the eccentric whole because sentences help the overabundance of the world cohere into something manageable, thinkable, graspable. Sentences are kind because they keep us company in this endless effort of which they may be a primary agent: they nurture continually this relation between a subject who says "I" and an object that says nothing at all.

Saint Augustine claims to recall aspect of coming into language and its powers. Of being an infant without speech, he recalls:

> Later on I began to smile as well, first in my sleep, and then when I was awake. Others told me this about myself, and I believe what they said, because we see other babies do the same. But I cannot remember it myself. Little by little I began to realize where I was and to want to make my wishes known to others, who might satisfy them. But this I could not do, because my wishes were inside me, while other people were outside, and they had no faculty which could penetrate my mind.[1]

This memory, given to him by others, sketches out a life common to each one of us but available to none. Augustine suggests that the infant is filled with wishes he cannot express, caught not simply in desires unfulfilled but, more darkly, trapped within an existence that has no outside, a center with no periphery, no others, so that the sum reality of the world exists within the limits of this one who feels but cannot say what is felt. The infant is somehow profoundly alone, living within the wishes inside him, unable to penetrate the nature of his own mind just as others find it also impenetrable. He can do no more than exist to himself until others can exist to him, until some force enters and realigns desire in such a way that the eye ceases to open only inward and instead gazes out. That force for Augustine is language:

> The next stage in my life, as I grew up, was boyhood. Or would it be truer to say that boyhood overtook me. . . . I ceased to be a baby unable to talk, and was now a boy with the power of speech. I can remember that time, and later on I realized how I had learnt to speak. . . . For when I tried to express my meaning by crying out and making various sounds and

movements, so that my wishes should be obeyed, I found that I could not convey all that I meant or make myself understood by everyone whom I wished to understand me. So my memory prompted me. I noticed that people would name some object and then turn towards whatever it was they had named. I watched them and understood that the sound they made when they wanted to indicate that particular thing was the name which they gave to it, and their actions clearly showed what they meant. . . . So, by hearing words arranged in various phrases and constantly repeated, I gradually pieced together what they stood for, and when my tongue had mastered the pronunciation, I began to express my wishes by means of them.[2]

Augustine offers a strange map to the working of the mind in language, a quality, I'd like to suggest, wonderfully attuned to the work that sentences accomplish in us and on our behalf. Learning to speak ushers us not only into the human community, and so integrates each of us into a social realm of shared values—the utmost of which might be the fundamental assumption of a reality all share and the ethical obligations that follow of the self in relation to others—but also introduces us to those two elements forged so deeply down in the human psyche: memory and desire.

"So my memory prompted me," Augustine says. In so saying, he makes us aware of an aspect of sentences that, regardless of the sophistication of the writer, cannot help but speak itself within our prosaic life. A sentence is an engine of desire. It calls out into the world from the echo chamber within us of all that we lack, and the world answers back as does a mother to a child's cry, fulfilling what it can. It is desire of a particular sort, a recognition so basic as to lurk underneath awareness, some peristaltic motion below even grammar's laws, this chthonic fact of appetite that is satiated only to want again with the same urgency. This repeated motion of desire, this force that propels subject through verb to object over and again, this momentum almost wholly oriented toward the future that so exacerbates the nature of our want, works by memory, by the backward glance, by all that time has stored away in the vaults of the desirous mind. The dark, forward grope of wanting is lit within by time already past that gives names to nameless wishes.

Such, I've come to suspect, is the kindness of the sentence—and by "sentence," I mean specifically this group of words in prose, something distinct from the line and different from the "poetic sentence." The sentence introduces us to our condition but does not abandon us to it. The sentence keeps us company. I want to think there is some sympathetic magic at work in honest language, maybe something akin to prayer but less lofty, directed only at the things of the world, the wants of the self, the reality of others. Within that sympathy that risks the utterance of wish because it has become so sure in its fulfillment, the fact of our mortal nature remains, reminds. The sentence, like us, has an end. Time moves through it even as desire does, following close on each word's revelation as a shadow follows close upon a body. Sentences don't repudiate what we ourselves cannot escape: that we want, and we are temporary. We want because we are temporary—and with us a sentence wants, wants with us, and is co-temporary, and comes to an end.

2. The Line

The line of a poem also depends upon memory and desire, and yet, beyond the simple difference of fragment and line break, beyond its resistance to closure, it seems to have a different life than does the sentence. Augustine, despite not only learning to speak but also in becoming a teacher of rhetoric and then a writer of many volumes, finds himself as an adult in curious parallel to his infancy:

> But many people who know me, and others who do not know me but have heard of me or read my books, wish to hear what I am now, at this moment, as I set down my confessions. They cannot lay their ears to my heart, and yet it is in my heart that I am whatever I am.[3]

A man who has become famed for his eloquence, for the mastery of his tongue, finds that he is unable to offer to others those words that might give image to who he is at the moment. One begins to feel, pondering the passage, that the descriptions we give of ourselves, and so perhaps of most things, are so riddled by time past that the sentences come to us as memories already made, and the present moment which they are meant to capture abandons the sentence at the utterance of its first syllable. Impossibly, we may live in time already past. Here the heart has a language all its own, speaking to itself in such quiet tones that Augustine might often be at pains to hear what it is it says and so learn who in this moment he himself is. The heart becomes an alternate mind, filling with memory just as it fills with blood. The rational, prosaic mind strives to overhear the heart in its ponderings, how memory in the other differs from memory in itself, how desire afflicts both—but desire too differs.

Enchanted by the way in which memory gives as present that which is missing, Augustine writes:

> Even when I am in darkness and in silence I can, if I wish, picture colors in my memory. . . . And while I reflect upon them, sounds do not break in and confuse the images of color, which reached me through my eye. Yet my memory holds sounds as well. . . . If I wish, I can summon them too. They come forward at once, so that I can sing as much as I want, even though my tongue does not move and my throat utters no sound. . . . I can distinguish the scent of lilies from that of violets, even though there is no scent at all in my nostrils, and simply by using my memory I can recognize that I like honey better than wine.[4]

These recollections bring back to the senses the physical realizations that years ago they first woke Augustine to—the ear fills with sound and the eye with color. These experiences must be so deeply embedded in the memory as to exist in some sense before the self-as-such. It is as if one learns to say "I" only after the taste of honey fills the mouth. More than a word, one becomes oneself, becomes an *I*, only after the heart has filled itself with lilies and song. There is no bewilderment dearer to poetic experience than the overwhelming sense of coming into a world that exists before I myself do—there fact and wonder are indecipherable.

It might be in such a place that the ongoingness of our infancy ceaselessly continues to exist. Augustine is of the same suspicion: that in his heart are those words that mark the moment, this *now*, whose reality separates itself from temporality. The desire that there exists does so not in order to be satiated but to feel as immediately as possible all that is and is not us, this desire that orients us back to reality of the world as a value eclipsing the mere fact of our own. Where as infants Augustine envisions us filled with unspeakable wishes, in this other vision of our ongoing infancy, we find ourselves as an inarticulate point within the articulate wish. We find ourselves witness to that wonder of the world that speaks itself into each mind through the senses of the body, work not of recognition but revelation.

Augustine describes this work in nearly elegiac terms—elegy being that broadest work poetry may be involved in. Wordsworth considers similarly when he suggests the poet is one who finds in absence, presence, and in presence, absence. Emerson, too, offers a parallel vision when he claims that "each word was once a poem." Immanent in all these insights is a quality of poetic language that makes a line of verse seem a form of life. To the degree that any given word in a poem speaks out of that first realization of an object before it etches itself into consciousness, we find some portion of that timelessness inherent in the *now* of immediate perception relict and alive in verse. It is for this reason, perhaps, that Keats's voice is so complicated with irony as he describes poetry as "a friend to man" in his "Ode on a Grecian Urn." Though we live in a cultural age in which concepts of the eternal in art, the immortality of the soul, are most often found heaped in the slough pile of yesteryear's self-deceptions, such thinking forces us to consider seriously that to work on a poem is also to work in eternity. Keats, writing his ode on the urn as he felt the fever that signaled his own death approaching, feels the terrible irony of what it is to write lines to make a poem. Those lines speak back into the eternity contained in beauty with words interpenetrated with truth, share a portion of it by participating in it—and in astonishing, heartbreaking ways, exclude from its cold heaven the fevered life that created it. The poem miraculously reverses our original position. No longer are we the silent thing filled with unspeakable wishes. No. We are the speaking thing that holds in hand the object articulate that holds its secret wish inside it and will not let us in. We bear the weight of those sweet, unheard melodies; we do not hear them. Even when we speak the poem so as to make it sing, it sings more sweetly to itself, the poem; and to that self-sung song, we are deaf, though we seldom know it.

3. The Poetic Sentence

I suspect it's all too obvious where I'm going with these demarcations of memory and desire: some hope or some claim that the "poetic sentence" is one that combines the human company of the sentence with the eternal nature of the line. Obvious, maybe, but it feels worthy, truthful if not true. Not simply a hybrid, the "poetic sentence" is one that has the courage to undercut both the arts to which it may be devoted. To return to Keatsian terms: it uses beauty to tease us out of thought and thought to tease us out of beauty. It figures time only to preface eternity; fulfills desire only to make us feel more keenly what in wanting cannot ever be satisfied. It comforts our helpless realization of our own mortality by coming itself to an end, even as it hides from us imperfectly what we also know that it will outlive us and speak to others with the comfort it now lathes upon our anxious hearts and minds.

One sentence of Proust's has always felt to me exemplary of this double life:

> For this present object was the one I would have preferred above all, as I knew perfectly well, having botanized so much among young blossoms, that it would be impossible to come upon a bouquet of rarer varieties than these buds, which, as I looked at them now, decorated the line of the water with their gentle stems, like a gardenful of Carolina roses edging a cliff top, where a whole stretch of ocean can fit between adjacent flowers, and a steamer is so slow to cover the flat blue line separating two stalks that an idling butterfly can loiter on a bloom that the ship's hull has long passed, and is so sure of being first to reach the next flower that it can delay its departure until the moment when, between the vessel's bow and the nearest petal of the one toward which it is sailing, nothing remains but a tiny gap glowing blue.[5]

Proust challenges us to see in two ways at once: the whole horizon between two blossoms and the passenger ship involved in moving from one point to another, social, commercial, and the same stretch of ocean as something incommensurable but near, a radical shift in scale that makes of the butterfly something larger than a ship and fills its endless appetite by moving from blossom to blossom with the slightest flick of its wings. Mostly, though, I like to think of that "tiny gap glowing blue." I like to try to see it. In the poetic sentence we are given the same gift of vision: some gap glowing blue. It is in that gap that necessary forms of bewilderment occur. There the mind overhears the heart and the heart also listens; there eternity grows hungry; there time is patient with want. The poetic sentence teaches us to see that gap. It is no small feat, to learn to see absence, to watch as nothing for us begins to glow. There isn't a word for it, nor are there words, nor sentences, nor lines. But in the subtle dissonance of the poetic sentence we gain some access to that which in being expressed remains inexpressible, that hold open within it some absence filled with wish, and those wishes are in no rush to cross the gap they exist in. They linger, they mutter, they moan in tuneless numbers—and then they sing.

To Arrive in Zeno's Thought

Reverie-On, Thinking-In, Peter Gizzi's
"A Panic That Can Still Come Upon Me"

1. If-When, If-Who

There exists a chasm, though nearly imperceptible, between reason and rationality—despite the depth of its abyss, regardless of the extent of its span, every day, heedless, helpless, hardly noticing, with nearly every step we take, we cross and cross it again and again. Or so I like to think. More than a motion of body, it is a movement in and of mind. Though so often the current state of poetic culture chides that reader who wants to ask of any given poem what work it does, what necessity it bears, I cannot help myself from doing so. To merely watch language perform itself on the page bears that meager interest of watching a person's face—be it stranger or lover—as she thinks: something there is happening, we might feel, but I have no access to it. Quietly, subtly, just by holding this image in our mind, another person's face caught in that outwardly blank look of inward attention, we bring ourselves to a primary ethical crisis. Do I trespass? Do I assume? Do I feel jealous, spurned, knowing she is within herself in ways I cannot join nor enjoy? Do I risk asking her what she's thinking of and so dispel the vision?

Or do I see for myself with her eyes what in the dark, electric, recesses behind the eyes her eyes seem almost to fill with? Do I imagine in myself what I suppose she is imagining and so possess for myself the vision that had been her own? If so, what of this experience is mine?—the face with thinking on behind it.

Stranger still, to be brutally honest, to confront myself not in my self-knowledge but all I know of my own ignorance—should I stare at my face in the mirror, would I feel the same mystification, some banal horror, that to my own mind my access is just as obscure? Do you wonder, as sometimes I do, that the very page the poem is printed on is just such a mirror, and in watching another mind go through the work of thinking, I see demonstrated back to myself the dark difficulty of doing the same? Do we gaze into the face of the thinking page and learn to think ourselves, or do we find that rational desire to discover the shared point of expressed connection severed by reason's ever-inward obscurity? And yet—

And yet, against this labyrinthine blank amazement of consciousness, as Peter Gizzi shows, as he knows or strives to know, "we ask that every song touch its origin / just once."[1] We do this asking in words that torment the boundary between inner life and outer expression. Origin opens the fundamental paradox of Gizzi's vision in the long poem that opens his collection *The Outernationale*. Perplexing and illuminating, the entirety of "A Panic That Can Still Come Upon Me" revolves around the ongoing crisis of source, of origin, an idea insisting that every utterance both mimics and repeats some first utterance, some initial calling out that not only pulls from within the mind those thoughts gathering to themselves the awkward garments of words, but also mines through the inchoate echoes of perception and memory that urge the world forth into cosmos. Origin in its deep paradox lives so deep within us and our songs that it feels true to say that it exists outside of ourselves—but it is an outside found only within. The poems I love most bear this audacity: they risk becoming the thing they pursue. In seeking to touch origin just once, a poem cannot help but become—just once—an origin in and of itself. I might call this work "devoted betrayal." But maybe not. Maybe that's easy; maybe it's coy.

Peter Gizzi begins his poem: "If today and today I am calling aloud."[2] The simple line opens us to complexities. "Today" posits *now*, the given world in a span of time, and so our ability to experience it, to wander in it, to have something of it, some proof stored away in nerve or mind. Its relation to time is reasonable, adding to the storehouse of individual experience so easily, if so erroneously, labeled "fact." But here "today" doubles. At once, "today and today" offers a sense of urgency, as if repetition creates insistence. It also implies sequence: that the second "today" is not the same as the first, but each day is a source of itself, a new *now* that requires the same call to be given not merely again but again for the first time; the position of the singer is to sing always the same song for the first time. Lastly, with more difficulty, "and today" posits within time another time, a day within the day, a repetition uncanny in its placement that suggests simultaneity and containment both: the other world that is, as Paul Eluard suggests, found only within this one. Adding to the Talmudic depth of the initial "calling aloud" is the phenomenological work the line knows it must accomplish. Evoking the ancient invocatory mode, it also marks within it difference, for here the call is without end, to no god or goddess, but instead, in the very language of its own utterance, these words must create the world in which their cry can be heard. Gizzi ushers us into a poetic mode that is deeper within us than memory can chart; and then subtly, honestly, ethically, creates shades within that bright archaic light, revealing not only that an ongoing relation with origin lives within this day of our living but also that another day lives there too. The day in the mind. The day of the mind. Reason's viceroy that precedes the beginning of the ancient song with the philosopher's most basic word of conditional conjecture: *if*.

That word *if* undermines the reality it posits, and hearing it, we feel that specific kind of doubt best described as conceptual realization. I can imagine it, I have an idea about it, a conceptual range in which it is true, but what is the reality of such ambiguities, such etherealities? Unlike more immediately poetic imaginings, *if* connotes the world of logic. We hear, it cannot be helped, some theoretical *then* biding its time in reason's anteroom, twiddling its conceptual thumbs, just waiting for the cue, after the comma, to make its appearance to muted, if still relieved, applause.

But not here. Gizzi holds off that reflex of the reasonable mind. He offers us no *then* but, more necessarily, more beautifully, only a *who*, only a *when*. In doing so, he opens a space of consideration in his poems that very few poets are capable of creating. He lets thinking become something another can enter, a work so intimate as to verge into the erotic (if by the erotic we can understand the absolute crisis of the ethical, point of greatest reality not of ourselves but the sought after and loved other). Within the cogs of reason, he points out the asymptotic distance that cannot help but threaten the gearing of logic's *if-then* clockwork. He pushes us into that imperceptible chasm and, as a poet must, accompanies us in our fall. There we experience that which poetry alone might offer us who love it, who feel we must continue to learn how to love it, who enter into the page not for the comfort of intimacy but the difficulty of it: that break where every *if* tends toward a *when*, where each *if* reaches toward a *who*, and reason is replaced by rationality. That *ratio* within rationality reminds us of the need for each one of us to continually renegotiate the relations that keep us connected to all that in our "unhappy discovery, too late to be helped,"[3] we've come to find is real: that *if* we exist, we exist. And so does the world.

Gizzi's repeating *if*, prevalent in the poem's first section, but also its dominant prosody throughout, posits at the far end of conditional conjecture actual being. He casts us into a necessary form of doubt (the very marker of poetic faith *rather than* that which must be suspended to be poetically devout) whose beginning pushes out from hypothesis into this astonishing if unsupportable fact: that the end of poetic possibility is nothing less than ontology. When the poet calls out aloud, "today and today," the teleology reaches past the bounds of logic and promises the *who* and the *when* of not yet encountered actuality. It as if we have learned, so the poem has taught us, how to step into the face of the thinking other—not a trespass but a kind of inevitability, if not an entire invitation.

2. Solar Sincerity

To find we "have arrived in Zeno's thought" steps us into eternity even as it crashes us into the day.[4] Zeno saw, millennia ago, that time presents us with a crisis we cannot escape. Not mortality. Death is not an event of life. Of it, we can reason; but to it, we have no rational connection. Time's crisis—or our crisis in time—bears itself out in Simone Weil's thinking: time doesn't exist; we live in time. Of the arrow sprung from the taut bow, Zeno realized that even as it coursed through the singing air, it would never, could never, hit its mark. Taken in any instant of its flight, the arrow is caught in the ever-decreasing distance between its point and the object of its aim. Living in time, we see the arrow pierce its target. Being within this other time that doesn't exist, we can glimpse that infinitesimal gap nothing can cross that exists between us and all with which we're in relation. Then we glimpse the arrow in its rational life: the arrow that is still even as it flies. Time hurtles its barb toward us, and we suffer this impossible harm of always being caught in the safe forever of being about to be struck and finding, even as we realize it cannot be wholly true, that we already bear the wound.

Gizzi puts us into such paradoxical motion because he so adroitly sings its qualities. Against the personal, so bound by time that he finds "our loves are anointed with missiles / Apache fire, Tomahawks,"[5] he sings also from the impersonal vision, where "sunshine hits marble and the sea lights up."[6] More so than Zeno's arrow, light alone is that piercing principle by which our open eyes, every instant of waking, are wounded. The syllable *sun*, the syllable *sea*, sung at the first moment of conscious realization, inscribe within their own utterance that fugitive *now* that contains within it its own undying source. Simultaneously, we recognize, we remember, we recall through the mind's vast storehouse those images of like experience that in our own minds provide some timely match, some sense of experience not as original but similar, familiar, a reasonable approximation, and the near-mythic spell dies. Gizzi's *if* creates in the opening, longest section of "A Panic That Can Still Come Upon Me" the profound ambivalence of sincere poetic experience: an arrow that in stillness flies, a world that is and is not, time's own agony, the eye open to the sun's light, and the I that in that light by others may be seen.

Light and time—light that is particle and wave at once, time that exists and does not—infuse the second section of Gizzi's poem with strange measure of perception:

There are things larger than understanding

things we know cannot
be held in the mind

If the sun throbs like a drum
every five minutes

what can we do with this

the 100,000 years it takes a photon
to reach the surface of the sun

eight minutes to hit our eyes

If every afternoon gravity and fire
it's like that here

undressed, unwound[7]

The eye, the organ most attuned to the instant, sensitive in its periphery to the slightest animal motions and light so dim that some stars can only be seen out of the corner and disappear when looked at directly, encounters the very moment only by utilizing a medium so ancient that each particle of it contains more time than the whole of human history. Gizzi sees that to witness anything—be it "nothing save Saturdays at the metro" or "the auroras' reflecting the sea"[8]—unfolds within the lived moment a span of time so large as to reach back past the mind into some mythic origin in which minutes, hours, and years exist in such overabundant supply that to measure them would be a fool's reasoned effort. If we learn to see truly, and if we can admit the unfashionable truth that we still turn to the pages of poems in order to accomplish just this good—work of seeking clarity, work of seeking cosmos, and in so doing seeking order—then vision becomes not an experience that occurs *in time* but something stranger, more essential, nearly magical, in which sight itself is filled with time, overflows with time, and any given image that fills the eye does so, for all intents and purposes, eternally.

When we open our eyes, we see by a light that makes infants of us all. I want to call such light *sincerity*, if by that word we can hear not a tone, not a style, but a focus—as of sunlight poured through the intensifying curvature of a lens (and so the open eye, just such a lens, finds a way to inscribe in the mind what it sees, as a child burns his name with a magnifying glass onto wood). Robert Duncan, in *The Truth and Life of Myth* (from which the title of Gizzi's poem derives), speaks toward the necessity of the poet to see according to such sincere light: "The roots and depths of mature thought, its creative sources, lie in childhood or even 'childish' things I have not put away but taken as enduring realities of my being."[9] The open eye, ever awakening to its own enduring infancy, must be the blossom that feeds the deep root that, in refusing reason's dark self-sufficiency, grows the ratio that connects the bright sun to inner thought.

And yet—

3. A Panic; or, Built in the Gap

And yet, Gizzi's poem strives for honesty, humility, where an easier route might seek "wisdom." As Duncan praises Socrates because "he knew he did not know," Gizzi too holds himself within the bounds of his knowledge so that he can all the more feel the limit beyond which knowing ceases. Over the course of the first three sections of "A Panic That Can Still Come Upon Me" a gradual drift taken place, one nearly infinitesimal, almost asymptotic, as hard to discern as the gap between reason and ration, seen first, maybe best, in the difference between the first line of the poem, and its variation that opens section three: "If today and today I am speaking to you, or."[10]

Against the first section's "calling aloud" which signaled invocation and so opened within the poem's initial gestures that ushering in of mythic time in which time-as-such seems not to pass at all, here Gizzi diminishes, deflating the ancient, epic gesture down into the human scale of "speaking." The word implies social intimacy, asserts the political and personal realities that bind us together and that depend on speech as a shared construct of creating interpersonal harmony. The poem widens the scope of its relational, rational life past the mythic epistemology of the poem's initiating crisis while not repudiating it. Gizzi's particular genius may well reside in such subtle shifts—felt best in how that pendulous "or" gathers within itself contradictory possibilities without negating the first. He moves the poem away from those philosophical paradoxes inherent in finding "we are still in motion / and have arrived in Zeno's thought" not as a departure but to show more thickly, more complexly, the ways in which no area opened in a poem is able in the same poem to be abandoned.[11] Gizzi holds himself to a kind of fate. It is a fate of the poem, a fate of the poetic page, in which Form as a metaphysical reality (more than form as an act of prosody) requires that every word establish a fact from which the poem can find no honest escape. Within the difficulty of such an idea, we brush again against the type of paradox Zeno establishes as part of the impossible order of the actual world.

A poem is, in its way, similar to Zeno's arrow. The song in every moment of its singing reaches that socially intimate "you" to whom it is addressed; at the same time, it is caught eternally in that address to the nameless You whose intimacy resides not in the interpersonal but the impersonal. Gizzi's poem is but one stunning example of such work; a poet, as was Duncan, who realizes that the "poem that moves me when I write is an active presence in which I work."[12] If the point seems minor, it does so only because it gains its greatest meaning within the asymptotic infinitesimal interval the poem opens within itself as the boundary gap between mythic timelessness and daily life. There "every struggle ice-cream truck tinkle" interrupts "the cosmological."[13] Gizzi knows, and so he shows, that the poet dwells within the poem he writes and is subject to the world, and every law of that world, the poem creates. He is not some god removed from the reality he makes. The very crux of the poetic act requires that we take the meaning of *poeisis* (to make) as seriously as possible, for only through it do we come to the necessary impossibility of the poet's position: one is maker and made at once, creator and also created. Stranger still, the poet exists most essentially within the work he's made: the poem. "Creative immediacy," as Duncan puts the effort of the poet's highest aspiration, inverts teleology in such a way that origins and ends intermix and cannot be told apart. Nor can one assume, as the reasonable *if-then* logic would assert, that cause precedes effect. Form subverts sequence in such a way—absurd as it may be, it feels most fair to say—that the poem precedes the poet.

And yet the poet within the poem doesn't reside in security, doesn't dwell forever in that eternity housed within its stanzas. The poem attunes the poet to the dangers it manifests within itself: this world that is worlds, this singular plural, this place in which reality is invested by imagination and made more real for the fiction. Duncan writes: "In the world of saying and telling in which I first came into words, there is a primary trouble, a panic that can still come upon me where the word no longer protects, transforming the threat of an overwhelming knowledge into the power of an imagined reality, or abstracting from a shaking experience terms for rationalization, but exposes me the more."[14] Gizzi's poem is written within this panic. His *if* creates the nervous ambivalence inherent in Duncan's primary trouble. Rather than try to resolve that crisis, Gizzi allows us to experience—through the gift of the poem creating the experience it suffers—what it is to be "bound by the most ignoble cords / if squatting in time."[15] The tension of those cords pulls taut by the rational connection between the world of myth and this one in which, like squatters in an abandoned house, we take our impermanent residence until the author kicks us out. Duncan feels the terrifying strain in which knowing and imagination fray and pull apart—a place in which the grounds for keeping the ratio between unlike worlds in relation dissolves. That fear then sentences daily life to the mere drudgery of time's indifference. The same fear lets us live merely fictional lives unconnected to the actuality that must—for life to be a substance poetic—interfuse and confound thinking, feeling, imagination. But to live within the panic is to refuse to allow the ratio to break, and it is there, as Gizzi writes, where "these gaps I feel are also the gaps / I am built inside."[16] He has gained the feel of not-to-feel, that Keatsian ideal that also is Keats's highest reality, in which the subject hovers before us divorced from subjectivity, sensing absence as actual, negatively capable, in which perception turns apperceptive, and to feel gaps within oneself is also to discover oneself in the gap.

4. I Am a Bridge I Am Standing On

It is within perception that the fourth section of "A Panic That Can Still Come Upon Me" opens:

A branch and the scent of pine in summer
the bridge and the water in the creek
the stones and the sound of water
the creek and my body
when hair and water flowed over me[17]

Each subsequent line moves through a different sense: smell, sight, sound, touch. In this turn toward a more traditional lyric mode, one that finds in its own history a means of escaping the philosophical paradoxes that torment the entire poem, Gizzi gives us what we thought could no longer be our own: the immediacy of the nervous body as the very base of our epistemological life. The world he describes is discovered in the mind via the senses that bring it to him, and the one omitted sense, taste, finds presence in the orality of the words themselves, bearing in them the sensuous nature of what they name. The body is immersed in the material it discovers, a unity with the world reminiscent of the eye opening always to its infancy. We find ourselves, as does the poet find himself, at the midpoint between those mythic ur-parents whose authority in the deep recesses of our minds still reigns supreme: father-sun and mother-earth. Just to sense the world one is in is to be an obedient child.

But thought rebels—even if it does not want to do so. That conditional syllable, *if*, returns—significant, increasingly so, of the inner life of mind that pivots from the senses and their connection to the very stuff of the world to the resources stored in the mind's dark.

If I am a bridge I am standing on, thinking,
saying goodbye to myself
when I stood by the water in my life
thinking of my life, pine boughs
the hill next to water[18]

In curious parallel to the previous section in which "or" hovered at the end of the line, not in denial but in accumulation of alternate possibilities, so this "thinking" energizes the poem's deep crisis at the very point at which we hope we might have put it away. That crisis is nothing less than consciousness itself. It is as if by *thinking* alone that the body is lifted out of the water and put onto the bridge. Hints at the self gazing at its own image riddle the stanza. "I stood by the water in my life / thinking of my life" vacillates between deep interiority and a continuation of the landscape given us in the section's opening stanza.[19] In both cases—imagining myself so as to think about myself, or staring down into my own reflection in the water—we catch ourselves in this moment of trouble, one that happens so quickly as to be nearly unnoticeable, in which that old construction, *I think, therefore I am*, reveals not the unity of self but its doubleness.

But this same force of consciousness that removes us from the elements of which we think becomes the structure of our contemplative life and, in so doing, expands as it must the limits of those experiences that count as actual. A poem such as Gizzi's here offers profound example. "I am a bridge I am standing on" gives paradoxical image to our thoughtful, poetic condition.[20] Not only does the line imply that the poem must become the world it discovers just as the poet must be the bridge he stands upon, it speculates (for what certainty is there) that this thinking life is the one that, even if it lifts us out of the river, offers us that means of connecting unlike points together and making of the unified, immersive world something more vastly grand, the reality of the metaphoric one. That reality requires impossible bridges to be built over fathomless abysses. But to think that bridge is solid is to over-assume if not to miss the point entirely. For the bridge—if Gizzi's line is to be taken as literally as we must—is itself a nervous thing, constructed of the very perceptions whose drift into apperception removed him from the cool creek. This apperceptive life, that inward work in which the senses learn to perceive themselves, each in such inexplicable ways self-aware—sight that sees that it sees—creates that very complex of imaginative realization that is a furtherance of the actuality rather than a separation from it. Only then does our initial hope become manifest: that the work of the poem participates in the reality to which it also contributes. Then the moment of the day—say, the tinkling of the ice-cream truck—indeed is part of the cosmological.

5. Symphonic Dailiness Is Felt Order

In the final section, when Gizzi says simply, "I'm not stupid,"[21] we might hear in the declarative mode a humble realization beneath the tonal play. I hear, at any rate, the declaration of a mind knowing it works, even if it can posit that only in the negative, only in the colloquial, only in the bratty. The line sounds like the answer a middle-school child gives to a question he thinks below his intelligence. At the same time, it speaks in, and of, self-realization. Hidden within it is some extension of Keats's parable about the nature of soul creation:

> I will call the *world* a School instituted for the purpose of teaching little children to read—I will call the *human heart* the *horn Book* used in that School—and I will call the *Child able to read, the Soul* made from that *school* and its *hornbook*. Do you not see how necessary a World of Pains and troubles is to school an Intelligence and make it a soul?[22]

Gizzi's panic, inherited as it is from Duncan, is but another version of Keats's "world of pains and trouble." Unlike easier modes of poetic epistemology, such thinking never assumes that the soul, or the mind, or the human heart, are givens in the human condition. For Keats, the heart inscribed upon by the damage of the world is that book the mind comes to read, and when the words are understood, the soul begins. It might be that when asked by a teacher some question, say, "What is the color of the sky?" the soul would answer, appropriately enough, "I'm not stupid."

Hearing that line in such a way allows us to enter most fully into the achievement of Gizzi's long poem—though perhaps "achievement" is the wrong word. As Duncan describes hearing a teacher of his read Blake aloud, a poem undoes our expectations of what marks it as good: "What was important was not the accomplishment of the poem but the wonder of the world of the poem itself, breaking the husk of my modernist pride and shame, my conviction that what mattered was the literary or artistic experience."[23] So too does Gizzi's poem seek to break the husk of our pride; it does so by breaking the husk of its own. That break in pride allows the poem's thinking to become our own and, vice versa, allows ours to become its. We see behind the eyes of the other what those thoughts picture; we put on the voice, so to speak, as a child might put on a mask—except the magic of the poem is that the mask is worn behind the face, and its image ends up being our own.

Once again, that syllable *if* looms. The doubt it contains becomes a winnowing force just as it becomes the figure that damages the heart in such a way that the intelligence of the poet moves past the anonymous and beyond the personal to some soul-like entity that contains both at once, coexisting opposites. Such a poem seeks its power not to control the world it creates but, far more importantly, to open itself to those powers—mythic, cosmological, and daily, mundane—in which our basic sympathies must be continually reawakened to the magic they are most persuaded by. It is a magic of being within non-being, of time within timelessness, of actuality within image, where

There is my body and the idea of my body
the surf breaking and the picture of the wave[24]

Poetic Geometries

Moby-Dick as Primer to Creative Crisis

I. Chaos: An Allegory

To call *Moby-Dick* an introductory text to the varying qualities of obsession may qualify as a profound understatement. Before one picks up
the book and opens it, she knows in advance some semblance of what
it contains: a white whale and a captain so bent on revenge he will sacrifice his entire crew in the vain attempt to wreck his anger back upon it.
But for those readers who, as if entranced by Ahab's own magnetic spell,
find themselves saying, as Ishmael does, that I "was one of that crew,"[1]
the nature of obsession becomes a different course altogether: no longer Obsession 101 but, rather, an endless class housed in the humanities
but cross-listed with those lessons in the eternal vagaries that inspire
and bewilder in equal measure and to which the reader-as-whaler is
devoted. Obsession contains layers, depths that rise up to become surface and, shattered by attention, reveal a deeper deep beneath. To lend
to Ahab—this most infamously obsessive of characters in our literature—
the full complexity of the drive that so deeply marks him is to trust that
obsession hurtles past mere monomania, mere egomania, and cannot be
simply ascribed to the psychological. Obsession here runs afoul of the
categories that should contain it. Ahab, whose "torn body and gashed
soul bled into one another; and so interfusing, made him mad,"[2] suffers
a collision of opposites grown confounded—body and soul, mind and
heart, and even, in stranger, more subtle ways, the necessary difference
between what is to say "I" and one's given name. Obsession stirs up the
lees of such primary bewilderment. And so stirred up, that same bewilderment requires obsession to give order to phenomena that are remark-

ably resistant to category. To read *Moby-Dick* by its own light—and we must keep in mind that it is a novel about pursuing illumination—is to find ourselves obsessed with the nature of obsession. Not ever an end in itself, obsession dislocates us in ways a whaler himself is dislocated: a point on a surface of indefinite depth and breadth, a sentient mark, a feeling pip, immersed in the very element of experience without yet having a word to name it as such. Then we are, as is Ishmael, as is Ahab, as is every man aboard the *Pequod*, a constituent of chaos.

What may fascinate so deeply in *Moby-Dick*—and perhaps why it is among those novels most famously left unfinished by those who begin it—is a demand hidden within it that we reschool ourselves, that we have not mastered what we assume years ago we learned: how to read. What we tend to be unskilled at is precisely what *Moby-Dick* demands— that against the order language imposes on the experience it narrates, we must find a way to let chaos back in. We must admit what is hardest to admit: that the very system of consciousness by which we make the world cohere in such a way that we can communicate our sense of it to another is itself a system riddled with gaps, excesses, lacunae, variable darkness, held breaths, unlit oil, mystic marks, fathomless volumes, inspirations, and exhalations. To read chaotically admits to our condition upon the sea: held up by an element we cannot grasp. So of meaning, of word, of thought, and so of experience—they are, like water, everywhere and nowhere at once. Against Captain Peleg's weary suggestion that Ishmael can see all the world from any place he stands—"nothing but water, considerable horizon though"[3]—chaos returns us to a capacity for wonder. But wonder differs from our assumptions. Inclusive as it may be of spectacle and all that in the whale fishery marks it unique, it also reclaims our attention back to those minute differences within sameness itself—as if in the blankness of the page, as on the blankness of the white whale, we must learn to discern again those subtle shades within whiteness that so tax mind and eye to resolve them into any significance at all. But it must. Or both book and whale escape. They escape, as Ahab would remind us, into the "little lower layer."[4]

Absurd to suggest, and yet it feels right: to imagine the book and its hundreds of pages as ocean-like if not an ocean itself. It puts us in a whaling frame of mind: read the surface so as to gain sense of what lies below it. So fated is *Moby-Dick* as a text—that is, fated in the sense that Ishmael's narration of it occurs after the events described, and so time subtly is turned backward, moving ahead only into what has already occurred—that one feels that to read it truly, one must see through a page to all the pages beneath and read them each at once. Then the depth could grow clear, and what in its dark ink is being sought could be seen.

Chaos seems composed of those depths that compromise the methods used to categorize it. It resists the order it also dismantles. Though Ishmael warns us vehemently against seeing *Moby-Dick* as "a monstrous fable, or still worse and more detestable, a hideous and intolerable allegory,"[5] the very nature of the book and its main protagonists seem to require us to do so. Against those allegories whose less tolerable ratios insist a given character stand exactly for a given virtue or vice, the obsessive, chaotic allegory *Moby-Dick* presents skews the ratios into variety and abundance. That mob of simultaneous significances lurks in the word itself. Allegory is cognate with *agora*, Greek word for the marketplace, place of public gathering, and, earlier, threshing ground and place of choral dance and song. Such an understanding of allegory leads one to ask different questions. Not "what does Ahab stand for"? Nor "what does Ishmael"? Better to ask "what all under these names gathers"? "Who all exist in the gathering place of these names"?

Hearing his would-be captain's name, Ishmael is taken aback. To Peleg's reminder that "*he's Ahab*, boy, and Ahab of old, thou knowest, was a crowned king!"[6] Ishmael responds, "And a very vile one. When that wicked king was slain, the dogs, did they not lick his blood?"[7] Peleg pulls him aside, looks at him with startling significance, and says, "Look ye, lad; never say that on board the *Pequod*. Never say it anywhere. Captain Ahab did not name himself."[8] Such a name bestows upon the one that bears it some aspect of the history it holds as a kind of fate, a relict of the past that impresses itself on the possibility of the inchoate future. Ahab grows into his name as one comes into inheritance, destined to some degree to ask those questions of how God might abide in the world with some sense that only blasphemous answers are courageous ones. Ahab gathers, so to speak, under his own name, hurtling along the lines his own hurt provides him, losing the distance so marked in most of us: that between saying "I" and one's given name there is a door ajar, to quote Dickinson, "just the door that oceans are." As if pulled together by a magnetic force so strong it collapses the opposite poles into a singularity, Ahab is

Ahab, through and through, and all of the crew are Ahabs too. The single straight line of the pronoun "I" links them, lines them up as one, a compass needle tuned not to north but to those depths down toward which obsession bends free will, helpless, heedless, a line that seeks its match in the depths of the Season-On-The-Line.

But in the tangled lines of chaos and fate Ishmael finds wrapped around him, these words of Peleg's contradict the reality of his own name. For Ishmael opens the novel by declaring the opposite fact: "Call me Ishmael." His name he has chosen. And who gathers there but all those who, bereft of their inheritance, find themselves unmoored in the wide wonder-world? Each of them nameless, for their names, as did our narrator's, drowned, drowned, and only "I" survived. No, not *I*. Just me— object not subject—just *me* survived. Every *me*, that is, whose self has been so stove by whale or world that we are returned to our primary philosophic position: trying to fix a leaky boat while on the sea afloat. And for those who gather in this allegory, each one of them is me.

What worries me most, what nags at the tangled yarn of my mind, are the ways in which Ahab and Ishmael might offer guidance into the work that has occupied the majority of my life: this making a poem. Beyond providing a subject, *Moby-Dick* ushers us back into the chaotic nexus that precedes chaos, that untamed, aqueous, breathless nothing that unworlds world in such a way that to speak, to write a verse, to write a sentence, reenacts the basic crisis of creative effort. Not to make a word but to forge a world. Ishmael and Ahab are bound together by more than a name on a contract. Each man offers himself as an archetype of how creative work is necessitated by the tragic sense of the world slipping back into chaos. Each one is lost in the infinite; each must find a method to limit what threatens them with limitlessness. Each must find a way—as each of us who read know we must too—to face the faceless white blankness of whale and page and just there to survive, make a mark. Both Ahab and Ishmael strive to do so, and each succeeds in differing, if partial, ways. Together, though, bound by crisis into their spurious condition, they might offer a would-be poet a means by which to make a hold within meaning itself. Not a permanent hold. Just a stay, just a delay, in which world holds on as world, air separate from sea, breath held and breath breathed, for a little while longer. *Moby-Dick* might introduce us to what tools are most distinctly our own in this whaling, wording work.

What does it take to make a world? Maybe nothing more than a circle and a line. Such simple poetic geometries just might underlie the whole delicate edifice of what we know and how we know it. The scholar thinks a building is made eternally solid; the whaler knows the foundation trembles; the whaler knows there is work to be done.

II. Ishmael; or, Circles

Only such a soul-spar could write as Ishmael does. Only Ishmael, naming himself after Abraham's first-born son, but son born to the wrong woman, could write chapter 32: "Cetology." In attempting to write a brief encyclopedia of all that of whales can be known, Ishmael returns us to the site of primary poetic crisis. A former teacher, he attempts to rely upon a system of knowledge he also knows he's abandoned by shipping aboard the *Pequod*. In comparing whales by their size to books by theirs—*folio, octavo, duodecimo*—he forges an implicit link between the two, suggesting a shared vitality, not only that whales are some strange compendia of knowledge but that books are also a form of life that dives fathoms down past the mind's reach. Even as we hold it, it escapes. The entries, as a species of definition, seek accurate portrayal. The promise of such work is an architecture that holds, an epistemology in which the words that lead us to imagine what they name do so precisely; and so the reader can, as the whaler must, rely on the knowledge imparted as an experience equivalent to life itself. But Ishmael knows the system fails, cannot be perfected. He comes to some sense that the line as a unit—be it a whale-line or that line of words, a sentence—runs short of the length needed, lacks the requisite strength, to pull up what it would name into fact. Meaning drifts away from proof into realms more poetic, depths in which language works in ways other than categorically, seeking not to classify whale or world, but more beautifully, to participate, to enact, to mimic instead. Such effort requires the abandonment of one technology for the use of another. Ishmael lets go of the line to pick up the circle.

To do so requires a strange initiation into one form of self-abandon. Aboard Starbuck's boat for his first lowering, a mate known for his caution in avoiding unnecessary dangers, Ishmael pursues a whale while a squall comes up and, "running through a suffusing wide veil of mist" while the frenzied whale rolls and tumbles "like an earthquake" beneath the boat, finds himself introduced to the indistinct terrors of ambiguity. Queequeg's thrown harpoon just grazes the beast. Something about the work of whaling removes experience from itself, cuts in halves Descartes's *cogito*, so that "I think" is a "loose fish," free from the existential suspicion that "I am." Ishmael's *I am* witnesses air and ocean so intermingle that they cannot be told apart, and he immerses himself—whether by choice or not, it hardly matters—in the confusion. To do so forces him to recognize that the old order by which the world made sense, where opposites held their relation to one another, where consciousness made claim that felt true enough to be called real (say, that the ocean is made of water and the sky of air) no longer suffices. The cost of the wonder-world he has entered alters his relation not only to the world-as-such, but to himself. Both *I am* and *I think* are simultaneously true but each independent of the other, neither proving the existence of which they mark only a portion. This change is reflected in his position: sitting in water up to his knees, the boat flooded and seeming to float up as a piece of coral from the ocean's bed, the gale increasing its howl, and Queequeg holding at the prow of the boat a single lit lantern, "an imbecile candle in the heart of that almighty forlornness."[9] So Ishmael spends the night with Starbuck's crew. In the image we see how little light the mind casts back into the world of the whaler. It is a lantern lit not to guide but to gather; not to forge a path but to be seen. It belongs not to the man holding it but is a symbol belonging to each in the flooded boat equally—reason's flickering, fading hope. It doesn't say *I think, therefore I am*. It says, *I am; we all are; find me, each one of me*. Existence proves just an iota within all that threatens to submerge it and, so reduced, the imprint of what it is to say *I* transforms from a pronoun that implies the identical, the personal, and becomes instead something compound, oddly anonymous, shared. Rescued finally by the *Pequod*, Ishmael takes precaution and writes out his will and locks it away in his chest. The act bears meaning also at a symbolic level. He writes out of himself that power of will by which any given self accomplishes what he may do, locks it away, and becomes will-less as a "quiet ghost with a clean conscience."[10] His *I*, missing his will, grows porous; he has lost that wall of self-definition that keeps his innermost self apart from another's identity. He riddles himself into plurality. Like the Greek chorus, when he says I he says I for all.

Unlike the line of "breadthless length," the circle is a geometry that figures the insufficiency of any single point of view. It turns away; it turns to. Its coherency resides in no single point's sufficiency. The same can be said of Ishmael's narrative strategy. He finds voice not a place of certainty but of poetic abandonment. *I am* becomes a bewildered position. Ishmael, in the hints he gives of his life after the tragedy aboard the *Pequod*, shows us—quite beautifully[11]—the results of this shattering, this being made wild, this bewilderment. He says, "I myself am a savage, owning no allegiance but to the King of the Cannibals; and ready at any moment to rebel against him." This becoming savage relies heavily on the word's etymology, coming from *silva*, a man of the woods, of the wilderness. Ishmael has become gifted—as he must be, and as the narration of *Moby-Dick* is profound demonstration of—in managing every form of instability, from the "universal cannibalism" of the world that insists all is in some sense self-consuming, to the realization that we must be as wary of ourselves as we are of others and of all things. At the same time, we find ourselves in allegiance to those most significantly not ourselves; not to mark the difference but to drift into their existence as if pulled in by some undertow. Ishmael reveals a wondrous facet of the bewildered condition: that the place of abandonment is also the realm of invitation. It makes place for others within us to dwell. So does the circle as a poetic geometry.

We feel that poetic ingathering most distinctly in "A Squeeze of the Hand." Describing the work of squeezing the crystallized sperm back into fluid, Ishmael also offers a gloss on the circular poetic that undergirds his ethical and aesthetical vision:

> Squeeze! squeeze! squeeze! all the morning long; I squeezed that sperm till I myself almost melted into it; I squeezed that sperm till a strange sort of insanity came over me; and I found myself unwittingly squeezing my co-labourers' hands in it, mistaking their hands for the gentle globules. Such an abounding, affectionate, friendly, loving feeling did this avocation beget; that at last I was continually squeezing their hands, and looking up into their eyes sentimentally; as much as to say,—Oh! My dear fellow beings, why should we longer cherish any social acerbities, or know the slightest ill-humour or envy! Come; let us squeeze hands all round; nay, let us squeeze ourselves into each other; let us squeeze ourselves universally into the very milk and sperm of kindness.[12]

Ishamel discovers within the work of being a whaler an education the former pedant could hardly have guessed at; the little iron rail of the pronoun *I* has been bent pliant and back upon itself, making a circle where before there had been a line. The age-old advice of the Delphic Oracle, *Gnothi Seauton*, Know Thyself, has been put away as just another myth a land-lubber holds to. To be upon the ocean, not as a traveler but as one who works on its surface to learn of its depths, ignorance is the way forward, and the counterbalance to the knowledge that experience gives the whaler in his labor is the corresponding gift of self-ignorance, self-bewilderment, self-illiteracy. (Queequeg is a primary example of the lattermost condition.) At work with his co-laborers, sitting in a circle around the tun filled with sperm, Ishmael squeezes his sole self into the communal body, keeping liquid not only the sperm that, exposed to the elements of the world, solidifies but keeping liquid that germ of anonymous intelligence before identity has molded it into personality. Here labor is an act at once physical and metaphysical, social and cosmic. Ishmael, thinking of the vision such work provides, sees "long rows of angels in paradise, each with his hands in a jar of spermaceti." It is a vision magnificent in its betrayal of merest "reality"—essence outside of existence, as if the soul bore within its intangible boundaries the body into which, wisdom decrees, it had been imprisoned or stitched.

This sublime sociability—itself an image almost cosmic in its profound atavism, its demand that we return to a form of existence that precedes the solidity of self and the world self seems fated to negotiate—finds companion in "The Grand Armada." As in "A Squeeze of the Hands," labor is the precondition for privileged vision; if the witness is not a worker, then he is no witness at all. Queequeg strikes one whale among a multitude. The wounded creature tows them away from "circumspection" into an existence felt as "the delirious throb." The mind's wary speculation gives way to the heart's frenzied circulation. That wounded whale trying to outrace the mere point of its pain drags Starbuck's crew through revolving circles, each a pod of whales in calm orbit that steadies the ocean's waves into a placid, lucid lake. The whalers find themselves towed through the outer circles into the innermost fold, a cosmic center, a navel of the world. Young whales, tame as pets, would come up to the surface to be scratched playfully with the lances meant to kill them. Violence here opens some enchanted gate: the sacred circle opens and lets in the trespassers, not as enemies but as initiates. Wonder-struck, the murderous end of their intent dissolves just as, being squeezed, the solid sperm melts back into liquid.

> But far beneath this wondrous world upon the surface, another and still stranger world met our eyes as we gazed over the side. For, suspended in those watery vaults, floated the forms of the nursing mothers. The lake, as I have hinted, was to a considerable depth exceedingly transparent; and as human infants while suckling will calmly and fixedly gaze away from the breast, as if leading two different lives at the same time; and while yet drawing mortal nourishment;—even so did the young of these whales seem looking up towards us, but not at us, as if we were but a bit of Gulf-weed in their new-born sight.[13]

Queequeg fears as he peers down that he sees a line and a mere baby has been struck; yet what he sees is the umbilical cord—not a line of whaler's cruel *techne* but a line that is a partial arc of the whole circulatory system with which the whale had just moments before been one. The whalers peer down into a gaze that looks beyond them, up into the infinite ethereal orders from which, out of nothing, the fact of their lives emerged from chaos into order. What Ishmael says of the suckling whales might likewise be said of him: he lives two different lives at one and the same time. He is a man of experience learning the uses of the line; he is anonymous, free-floating, merging into the life of others as a shape of water moves into another shape, speaking as them their thoughts that otherwise would be, maybe forever, silent. Such circles of narration act, as does the lake formed in the whale's revolving cosmos, as a membrane, a lens—one not unlike the thinnest skin of the whale, wholly transparent, and that dried, exerts a slight magnifying force on the words of the books Ishmael reads—that allows not only the whalers to glimpse down into the sacred orders where life itself moves from essence to appearance but also allows the newborn creature to glimpse the indefinite realm from which its now mortal life emerged.

The circle as a poetic geometry acts just the same. It keeps porous the boundary line between distinct orders of existence, be it the horizontal, social relation of squeezing sperm or the vertical one of heavens to surface to depths. Seen through properly, the eye is one such circle; so is the pronoun *I* when it bends, ouroboros-like, and makes of itself a circle. The vision holds each man in its spell until a struck whale swims madly through those cosmic rings trailing a line with a loose harpoon slashing behind it, wounding others as he tries to flee the pain of his own wound. Then chaos of a lesser order reasserts itself: not chaos of source, of creation, but chaos of violence and death. I can imagine that line as dark as the line of ink the nib of a pen leaves behind. To make a point might also be a violent act; meaning might crash headlong through deeper forms of order. What harm is there in bringing any fact up into light?

What we know of Ishmael's later life, the one he lived after the tragedy aboard the *Pequod* but preceding, it would seem, the writing of this novel, echoes out from that question. The white man who—in the earliest chapters when he first sees Queequeg's markings—he has heard tattooed himself over his whole body, ends up, of course, being Ishmael himself. Strange forms of prediction abound in poetic circles, as if in attaching ends to beginnings, time itself returns to its cyclical, mythical, repetitions. Ishmael speaks of it quite movingly:

> The skeleton dimensions I shall now proceed to set down are copied verbatim from my right arm, where I had them tattooed; as in my wild wanderings at that period, there was no other secure way of preserving such valuable statistics. But as I was crowded for space, and wished the other parts of my body to remain a blank page for a poem I was then composing—at least, what untattooed parts might remain—I did not trouble myself with the odd inches; nor indeed, should inches at all enter into a congenial admeasurement of a whale.[14]

The body becomes the book, just as it had been for his bosom friend, Queequeg. What Ishmael knows he has marked upon himself so he will not forget it. But against the lines of measurement, congenial they may be, he has left open upon himself a blank space, a page open not for fact to fill but for a poem. I imagine that blank page hemmed in by the dark marks of ink that everywhere mark what experience has taught him. Knowledge forms the circle it cannot enter. And as Dickinson will claim of herself that "My Business Is Circumference," so we see in Ishmael a parallel wisdom. He has left a blank circle upon him. It is the space of ignorance that fact makes available but into which it cannot enter. Such is the poem's realm. It is not yet written. The whole novel is but a prelude to that still unwritten poem.

III. Ahab; or, Lines

How do you alter possibility into probability? How do you change possibility into certainty? You do as Ahab might advise. You use a line.

Emblematic of the man: his sleepless nights spent beneath a lamp burning on whale oil, head bent over the chart he studies,

> you would have seen him intently studying the various lines and shadings which there met his eye; and with slow but steady pencil trace additional courses over spaces that before were blank. . . . While thus employed, the heavy pewter lamp suspended in chains over his head, continually rocked with the motion of the ship, and forever threw shifting gleams and shadows of lines upon his wrinkled brow, till it almost seemed that while he himself was marking outlines and courses on the wrinkled charts, some invisible pencil was also tracing lines and courses upon the deeply marked chart of his forehead.[15]

Ahab's work on the charts, his "threading a maze of currents and eddies" with the line drawn from a pencil,[16] offers an image by which we can not only understand the peculiar *techne* of the line's poetic geometry but can also immediately apprehend its difference from Ishmael's circular nature.

Ahab seeks that point at which the line he draws will intersect the line of Moby Dick's undersea migration. His line works in depths even as it works on surfaces. The leaden line on the page traces down through fathoms in which no man can breathe but this man, this Ahab, can plumb, can plan, can plunder. This single line exists on multiple planes at once, insisting that what is below can, by force of its own mark, become that which is revealed above. Such a line is a means of capture within all uncertainty, makes into possibility that which, missing a line, would remain something even less than potential. What Ahab seems unaware of—and what Ishmael, with his circular, cosmic vision seems uniquely attuned to—is the parallel gesture, the invisible hand that charts upon him the very lines he draws on the map. As Ahab draws his line through the ocean's depth, so the depths of his mind are traced. So wounded is the man, of soul as much as of body, that extraordinarily outward effort of drawing one line certain through the ocean's illimitable depths finds unknown reciprocation in the most inward depths of his mind. Such a line does strange work to the eye that can see it. It implies that a wound metaphysical as it is physical cannot be stitched shut by mere thread; but a mere thread, wound through the amazement of word and wound, insists that inner and outer bear no difference and that thought, and faith, and belief, and doubt are likewise an ocean whose surface is but the wrinkled page of a man's brow. Ahab doesn't know it, but the line insists that the white whale (that swimming, living blank) will be found in the ocean only when it is also found in himself. And so of the tarred, hempen line tied to the thrown dart. It will be thrown within even as it is thrown ferociously out. The line seems to insist on metaphysical parallels—depths, surfaces, heights—that it also refuses to make explicit. Well, refuses until the lines all intersect. That's a point we call a wound.

"Accuracy," etymologically, is a form of care. It's a poetic realization in and of itself, that to be accurate is a kind of love. Ishmael is one, it should be noted, who is deeply attuned to the moral crisis of accuracy; he seeks to be as much so as he can be, and he offers critiques, humorous and profound, of those who have failed to accurately portray the whale. Ahab seeks something other than accuracy, nor should we assume that the line-as-such, the line as poetic tool, concerns itself necessarily with an accurate rendering of what it would name. For this man who feels his purpose "laid with iron rails, whereon my soul is grooved to run," the accurate line does contradictory work, attunes itself to excesses so grand they eclipse rendering, trace the monstrosity they're hurled toward, not to bring it up into some harmony of air but to find its vital place and there give it accurate harm. Perhaps it's easiest to see the point by an opposing example. Ishmael, kindly, gives us one:

> On Tower hill, as you go down to the London docks, you may have seen a crippled beggar (or *kedger*, as the sailors say) holding a painted board before him, representing the tragic sense in which he lost his leg. There are three whales and three boats; and one of the boats (presumed to contain the missing leg in all its original integrity) is being crunched by the jaws of the foremost whale. Any time these ten years, they tell me, has that man held up that picture, and exhibited that stump to an incred-

ulous world. But the time of his justification has now come. His three whales are as good whales as were ever published . . . and his stump as unquestionable a stump as any you will find in the western clearings.[17]

Ishmael, in quiet ways, makes many claims for the nature of art in relation to experience. Greatest inaccuracies occur, he suggests, in those renderings that derive from the mere distance of objective rationality; such paintings might capture an outline, but they do not offer a glimpse of the life that informs it. The accuracy of this *kedger's* painting of three whales derives from his being within the very squall of the hunt, within the quick of the crisis, from he emerged without whale, awfully scathed, and with only the ability to represent that which nearly killed him.

Lurking within these "good whales" is an aesthetic theory that secretly demonstrates itself throughout the novel. It insists upon a link that connects experience to experiment; that bond in *accurate* art is as strong as the nuclear bond within an atom. But such accuracy deriving from the lived experience bears within it all the ambiguity of life, all the entering into boiling waters to get as near as one can to what one wants. What one wants also wants to escape. It might take a limb with it as it goes. Against the clinical eye that profits most from lending to others a means of recognition, this whaler's accuracy inscribes within it the mortal dangers of what it is to want to make an image of the world. You must go into to it to do so. And this world that, as Heraclitus says, "loves to hide" has some vested interest in keeping dark what the line would make visible. Keats realizes much the same, bears within his poetic thinking a parallel aesthetic concern, when he says, "Do you not see how necessary a World of Pains and troubles is to school an Intelligence and make it a Soul?"[18] Why is the kedger's painting held up for ten years so he can make his living begging? Because it renders into lines the creature that in damaging him so grievously broke his intelligence and made it a soul. Unlike the scientists Ishmael finds so often at fault, this beggar achieves accuracy because he works from an ignorance that knows itself. Such is one gift experience gives. But I might argue that the painting is not what is most accurate. For the picture of three whales and three boats is itself in representative relation to the unpaintable thing, that which is there only by not being there, evidence that has absence only as its proof: the missing leg. It may seem like a small return, given the investment, but it's not. This whaler discovered a means of offering to others what he experienced himself; and in their recognition of its truthfulness, they give him coins, and he makes his way though the difficult world.

What the whalers we have become by reading *Moby-Dick* cannot help but recognize is that our captain has suffered the very same wound. But Ahab paints no paintings, draws no drawings: he sits at a table at night all night and draws lines in the ocean. To achieve any accuracy, the line must learn to betray itself, to work against the infinite reach of its own geometric nature. It must bend and circle back and join—as Ishmael joins— its end to its beginning, for only in circumference does a world become apprehensive. But Ahab's soul runs grooved on iron railings. The infinite in him rides straight along the line's poetic geometry: "length without breadth," yes, but also a means to pursue that which denies pursuit as a possibility: divinity, infinity, immortality, and the principal agent who creates such incommensurabilities that so tease the mind out of thought. Ahab has a line. It is his poem. It has no meaning because it has no words. To stop there would be to give up his mad chase. Then possibility becomes something more fearsome than certainty; it becomes fate. We're witness to that moment, that fatal error. It happens when Ahab speaks to us all for the first time aboard the quarterdeck. Here he must make his purpose known, must hawser his crew to his plan. He asks questions that derive from experience.

"What do ye do when ye see a whale, men?"[19]

One by one they answer, and the answers are right, so they please him.

Then he asks after a certain whale, if they've heard of this whale. It's a white whale. White as a snow hill. White as a page.

Tashtego says, "That white whale must be the same that some call Moby Dick."[20]

And Ahab hears the name, and in front of all, he asks, he doesn't say, he asks: "Moby Dick?" He asks it as if he had forgotten the name, or didn't know it. This man devoted to nothing less than killing this one whale in all the oceans in all the world has forgotten the name of what he pursues. Such is the counsel of the merciless line. Were Ahab to say the name over and again to himself, his point would pierce only an image—an image the name itself creates. He wants to "strike through the mask."[21] But to make the unspeakable wish of his heart known, even Ahab must speak. To wind his line around his crew, he must speak, he must say the name that he hates, and in saying it he must submit himself to representation, to the trap of accuracy, in which, by making the white whale visible to others he makes himself again visible to the whale. See, now, this fatal reciprocity of the line?

What do you do when you see it?

You sing out.

The mouth makes something like a circle then; and then the word on a line flings out.

What Kind of Monster Am I?

I imagine the heat of the day is building and puts a fever in the air. Cicadas sing from the trees beside the river in whose cool waters they walk, Socrates and Phaedrus. They are there with a third, though he cannot feel the current. He is rolled up and hidden in Phaedrus's sleeve, Lysias, speech maker, who gave Phaedrus, beautiful young man, a speech. The speech says one should give oneself to a non-lover and not a lover, for the non-lover will bring no harm to the beloved. Lysias is there with them, all rolled up, text replacing body, word containing breath but not breathing in the blood-hot air. Socrates follows those words; he wants to hear them read, for he is "a lover of speeches." As they walk down the river to a place he knows, where the grass is long and the flowering trees bloom, where a plane tree offers its shade, he keeps asking Phaedrus a curious question, interrupting the conversation: "Do I seem inspired?" The question thrills because it doubts where doubt cannot be felt. It insists that something as divine as inspiration can be but an appearance, even to the one feeling inspired. Socrates admits to a glorious confusion, one that is self-mocking and mocking of other at once. Just before they stop, just before the day has reached its noontime heat, Socrates admits the depth of his own ignorance—an ignorance excited into near bliss by the words soon to be read, that speech Lysias wrote down, anticipation nearly sexual. He says:

> I am still unable to fulfill the command of the Delphian inscription and "Know myself. . . ." Am I a monster more complicated and swollen with passion than Typho[n], or a creature of a gentler sort, naturally a part of some divine, and not monstrous, dispensation?[1]

Socrates's genius resides in him in such a way that it damages the solidity of the self. He feels his ignorance as a lover feels desire, and like a lover, his desire worries him, frets and frays self into selvage. He wants to know what kind of monster he is. Like Typhon, is he hundred-headed and from every mouth can he speak in every voice, using words to convince, to beguile, to seduce? Can he speak so as to mask his ignorance with knowing? Can he appear inspired? Or is he a monster of a gentler sort, a monster I might call a lover?

. . .

Anne Carson's *Eros the Bittersweet* ends as a loving consideration of the *Phaedrus*, this book that insists, as does her own, that writing and desire must be intimately interconnected, nearly one, if a reader is to become a lover. It is only on returning to her book that I realize its fundamental importance to me, though I long had felt its influence, the way one remembers encountering the necessity of something that cannot be wholly grasped—say, the scent in the air only after the flowers have been walked past. But returning I find this book has been for me the guide into how it is I want to read, a little lover's manual on the erotics of the page. How does the lover begin? The lover begins by breathing in.

Carson suggests a lovely mystery: How is it the poets who introduced their audience to Eros were also the first to write down their verse in letters? The fact beneath the subtle suggestion that lyric poetry helps create the desire it both invokes and suffers involves the nature of the Greek alphabet. Greek introduced vowels into the Phoenician system of writing, creating a method to record the nuances of sound in unprecedented ways. "A script that furnishes a true alphabet for a language is one able to symbolize the phonemes of the language exhaustively, unambiguously, and economically."[2] The written page could suddenly mimic the intimacy of the human voice, not only by offering phonemic clues to the words as they would be said but also by marking in them a figure of utmost intimacy, those vowels that contain the breath they are uttered by. A living principle of speech embedded itself in the written word: breath, *pneuma*, genius, soul. The written word has become a place of indwelling. The word, like the beloved, excites desire because, like the beloved, the word is ensouled.

Lyric epistemology creates desire. Carson writes, "There would seem to be some resemblance between the way Eros acts in the mind of a lover and the way knowing acts in the mind of a thinker."[3] Eros acts, as Carson notes, in paradox, that devastation of contradiction that is also a form of bliss. Desire seeks out the lack that births it, this need for the other that supersedes and overwhelms the need for the self to remain inviolate. Desire finds in the mind of the lover a resource of lack, a space of wanting that makes desire desirous. When knowing acts in erotic ways it discovers in the mind a similar insufficiency; it discovers an ignorance it deepens. The poem offers to one who reads it by its own paradoxical terms an unexpected difficulty: not acquiring knowledge but reaching into ignorance as the mind's primary resource; and by that reach, which, by going so far into the self it inverts and reaches out, one becomes that figure with outstretched hands, that figure of longing, the lover. The poem places itself between poet and reader as the world into which both must reach in order to become real. Just as Carson describes the source of the *symbolon* as "one half of a knucklebone carried as a token of identity to someone who has the other half,"[4] it feels that the poem is the place in which the half that is a reader meets the half that is a poet and on the page they consummate a wholeness. But as with love, there are consequences. Each half of a symbol reaches through a distance it also gathers into itself—a coiled spring of nothingness—so that the formation of the symbol includes within it a source of absence. The symbol contains in it the very force that will ruin it: the erotic distance of the lover's reach. It contains that distance as the vowel contains breath. To read is in part the lover's dream, that no breath other than what the beloved breathes out is needed to breathe in. To read also confronts the lover's great fear: that when the wholeness is done, when the poem has been read, when the mind steps out of the nuptial bed and over the threshold back into knowing, the distance crossed expands, and one must learn to desire more fully to experience again that pleasure within the written sheets.

What is this monster the poem creates? A hybrid one that in saying "I" means "we"? Aristophanes's myth of the lover's lack, where we want so heedlessly the love of another because we two were once one—two-headed and eight-limbed—an erotic whole so powerful it seemed within our reach to challenge the gods. Zeus took the threat seriously enough to sever each in half, so now I pick up the poem with two hands, and cross one leg over the other, and must begin love's work alone. Or are we Typhonic, as Socrates feared of himself? Each poem allowing us to alter our voice, to speak as anyone, to mimic the already-loved voices and so seduce by a heartless trick the one we desire? Or might my disposition be gentler? Might I need to become, brief as the time may be in which it occurs, this lover in the sense Carson offers—this *symbolic* creature, birthed only in the poem being read as it's being read, in which the opposition of reader and writer ceases as does the division keeping lovers apart? I'd like to think so. I do think so when I think *as* I desire; that is, when my thinking *is* desire.

The honest lover departs. He must do so to learn to desire again, to desire more fully, more truly. Carson makes us remarkably aware of edges in relation to Eros. She writes, "The self forms at the edge of desire."[5] If we read as lovers, if the poem opens within itself a place for that consummation called reading to occur, then when reading stops, only then, do we become that thing in which our ethical and our erotic lives are one. Only then am I me. The poem has granted me myself in giving me that lack by which I not only desire but also find in myself "desire for *desire*."[6] Such wanting reorients the reader to the world in that most remarkable of ways; it does so by introducing us to it and telling us, as does the beloved to the lover, that "sometimes I am permitted to return." A poem places a seed in unexpected ground. Not soil, not earth. It grows in nothing, takes root in nothing—that nothing desire deepens in us, that lovely emptiness of wanting. Right there it takes root. We find the startle of our moral life when we feel it begins within our erotic one: that the care of what *is* depends on the longing that springs from what *isn't*.

As Sokrates [*sic*] tells it, your story begins the moment Eros enters you. That incursion is the biggest risk of your life. How you handle it is the index of the quality, wisdom and decorum of the things inside you. As you handle it you come in contact with what is inside you, in a sudden and startling way. You perceive what you are, what you lack, what you could be. What is this mode of perception, so different from ordinary perception that it is well described as madness? How is it that when you fall in love you feel as if suddenly you are seeing the world as it really is? A mood of knowledge floats out over your life. You seem to know what is real and what is not. Something is lifting you toward an understanding so complete and clear it makes you a jubilant. This mood is no delusion, in Sokrates' [*sic*] belief. It is a glance down into time, at realities you once knew, as staggering beautiful as the glance of your beloved.[7]

Suffer beauty, says the poem to the one that loves it. Bear its thrill. Endure longing longer. What we could be may be perceived only by feeling what we most truly lack. Such is desire's bittersweet gift. Anne Carson encourages us into Socrates's belief because it feels to us who read her words that she herself is such a believer. We must learn to want if we wish to live fully, and our teacher in this is the words themselves, not the lesson they may impart but the fact of the breath in the vowel, that "mood of knowledge" that drifts upon us like an erotic reverie in which the soul seems larger than the body that contains it, and the eyes, when they open, open on desire itself, word and world, beloved's eyes, poet's mouth open in invocation, that one letter that contains the breath of the mouth that holds the shape of its last utterance: O—

Ghosting the Line

Susan Howe and the Ethics of Haunting

it must acknowledge the spiritual forces which have made it
—MARIANNE MOORE

Too much and not enough.
—HERACLITUS

Prefatory

I first read Susan Howe's poems in the springtime. A professor had given me a copy of *The Nonconformist's Memorial*, and one day when the sun shone bright and winter finally felt put away, I walked out from the ratty apartment I shared with my wife, walked across the street, sat under a tree, my back against the rough bark, and began to read. I read the entire book. When I finished, I turned back to those mirrored pages in "A Bibliography of the King's Book, or Eikon Basilike," the lines not behaving on the page as lines of poems were supposed to behave, lines crossing each other, clipping across each other's utterances, lines that confuse, lines that confound, that make of themselves a web in the eye, a nest in the eye, lines growing tangible as they grew tangent, not one voice but voices; I could hear them as if in a room in which words gained body, words putting themselves in this difficult and impossible grace called *delay*. Something meant to disappear had not disappeared here: the words of which voice is constructed, these "vibrations of air." These mirrored pages seemed to look at each other; when the book is closed, these pages lie with one face pressed to the face of the other, not a kiss but a kind of circular breathing, a kind of circulation. I looked and looked at those pages. I read in the middle—

t

o

v ip

   A

and on the facing page—

A

 pi v

   o

    t^1

the word broken apart letter by letter but legible through its damage. Here is one form of fearful symmetry: a pivot that pivots itself. See how the word isn't linear but in orbit around itself, a centerless center. But these two pages mirror each other, reflect each other. The word is not the only thing in circulation. It is as if one page looks at itself in the mirror, but neither page knows which is just an image and which is actual, nor does the reader know. There is a question here; it is not a question that asks itself, nor is it a question that can be asked. We feel the medieval philosopher's endless concern with the nature of the reality of the mirrored image. Except here it is not a face reflected, behind which could be seen the room in which the philosopher asks his questions of himself to himself, some self who will not answer but only mimes back the face in its effort. Here voice reflects voice, an echo chamber in a mirror on a page as still—one might hazard to say—as Narcissus's pond. Origin asks a haunted question: Am I the first?

Am I the first?—that is how I felt reading Susan Howe's poetry. It is the feeling of one who enters into the world and becomes bewildered. It is a wilderness condition. And when I looked up from the pages, I looked up into the tree out-branching above me. I felt like my breath had blossomed; and when I breathed in, I breathed in the whole tree.

Breath

The library is a forest, a woods, a wilderness. Leaves of trees and leaves of pages fall from branch and from binding fall. That hush in the dimly lit narrow between stacks? Don't mistake solemnity for the dead leaf–strewn path; don't mistake silence for those thinnest threads that voices trail behind them in their song. Even what is wild finds a trail and marks it more legible as it passes. Reading is when the eye falls on some compost the foot can't find. "Often a damaged edition's semi-decay is the soil in which I thrive," says Howe in her "Personal Narrative" in *Souls of the Labadie Tract*.[2] The damaged voice provides the fertile ground.

Invert the symbol and the library becomes ocean. Melville, quoted by Howe in *The Nonconformist's Memorial*: "But I have swam through libraries." Howe, too (like Coleridge), a "library-cormorant," finds in words' watery depths that which nourishes. There is also the book open and flat on the library's table, the pages gathering as two waves about to crash together (or is it a wave about to crash into its own reflection?). And Dickinson: "There is no Frigate like a Book."

To enter these woods recognizes that the "errand in the wilderness" is still our own, these woods through which voices run more swiftly than do the deer, these savage-haunted, prophet-hunted woods. To enter this ocean is to ship with Bulkington on Captain Ahab's *Pequod*, where "all deep, earnest thinking is but the intrepid effort of the soul to keep the open independence of her sea."[3] When Susan Howe walks into a library, she walks into the woods. In the "vocalized wilderness" she grows bewildered. It is a mark of honesty, this becoming lost, this losing one's way. When she dives down, she dies a little and also she denies death. A page is just a surface masking underneath it unfathomable depths. What does the poet-reader, library-cormorant do? She learns to hold her breath.

• • •

I have heard the wind blow through the woods in such a way that I thought the ocean was near. And I have smelled in the air blown off the ocean a fertile, fecund, rotting smell, as of leaves overturned in a forest. Wind plays tricks, and breath plays tricks too.

Sometimes by the seaside
All echoes link as air
Not I cannot tell what
so wanton and so all about[4]

The voice, Howe reminds us not only in *The Nonconformist's Memorial* but throughout the entire body of her work, is composite in the strangest of ways. A construction of opposites, a voice is word carried on breath, sound borne by silence. The voice lives "a sort of border life,"[5] and the border divides what it divides not flawlessly but with deep flaw. The voice keeps letting time escape into memory, moment into echo. The body of the word keeps breaking down into no body at all, a kind of silence that is also a kind of soul. The voice marks that border where oppositions fail to be opposite, word and world, syllable and silence, body and spirit. The voice found on the page—that ocean-like blank formed of the forest's wood—navigates a wilderness it contains within itself. It bears in it the marks of "The literature of savagism / under a spell of savagism,"[6] where, here, *savage* shakes free of connotation and returns to Thoreau's etymology, traced from the Latin *sylva*, dividing in Old French and Middle English into *sauvage* and *salvage*, the latter meaning simply *a person of the woods*. Pages are savage. Words make the trails they mark. To read is to enter the woods, and to enter the woods is to become bewildered. Howe: "Who is not a wild Enthusiast."[7]

But the enthusiast wilds herself at more than the music inside the voices she hears. She hears also in the voice that the voice cannot speak, the silence the voice contains, marked by no words but by the breath words contain within themselves, some blank instant some call now and some call forever. Thoreau, January 4, 1851: "The longest silence is the most pertinent question most pertinently put." Howe is a poet uniquely suited not to answering this most pertinent question but, through the border life of the poetic voice, letting silence ask its ongoing question within her own words. It is a question by which she brings herself into question. Thoreau again:

My life at this moment is like a summer morning when birds are singing. Yet that is false, for nature's is an idle pleasure in comparison: my hour has a more solid serenity. I have been breaking silence these twenty-three years and have hardly made a rent in it. Silence has no end; speech is but the beginning of it. My friend thinks I *keep* silence, who am only choked with letting it out so fast. Does he forget that new mines of secrecy are constantly opening in me?[8]

Thoreau sees that to speak is to speak silence, speech being but silence's beginning. A word strangely reflects the crisis of body and soul. A syllable marks not only the initial sound as it builds into sense; it also marks exactly where time seems to begin. And because of time, suddenly there is history, suddenly there is history in all its suddenness. But the voice is carried in breath's silence; but the voice carries within it that silence on which it is borne. Words contain within themselves that breath that is silence without end, silence larger than the word that contains it—a silence that does not deny expression but affirms it. That breath affirms that chaos still dwelling within cosmos.

Words are an illusion
are vibrations of air
Fabricating senselessness
He has shattered gates
thrown open to himself[9]

When the word is spoken, when the illusion ends, one is left with the senseless air alone. One has put breath, then, into one's breathing— shattered gate of one's own mouth, one's own mind. That breath is not simply one's own. That breath is not simply the air in the lungs.

Such silence marks the curious terrain of poetic perception. Giorgio Agamben offers to bring such silence into consideration:

Not only memory . . . but also forgetfulness, are contemporaneous with perception and the present. While we perceive something, we simultaneously remember and forget it. Every present thus contains a part of non-lived experience. Indeed, it is, at the limit, what remains non-lived in every life, that which, for its traumatic character or its excessive proximity remains unexperienced in every experience.[10]

Howe, who knows to ask through the work of the poem about that toward which the poem itself works, writes in the "unutterable gathering darkness" where "I stray to stray[11]," toward that *who* "Who is this distance / Waiting for a restoration."[12] It is too simple to say that this poetry's relation to history is one of reclamation and recognition—of bodying the ghosts—for Howe's poetry contains in it the full complexity of memory occurring in the moment. It arrives in its experience containing that which cannot be experienced. Howe speaks her invitation, her voice in which voices might reside, the poem a place of dwelling not unlike the library's wilds, where, the poet says, "I am at home in the library / I will lie down and sleep."[13] Howe does this work—a work not wholly unlike how sleep bides in the midst of wakefulness—of bringing herself, and so bringing her readers, into that "excessive proximity" that remains silent, experienced only through the fact of its resistance to experience. She offers what remains "not-lived in every life" and whose spiritual nature belongs, as Howe writes of it, to the "Occult ferocity of origin."[14]

Breath, I mean to say, is an origin. Breath occult in every word. We forget we are speaking silence when we speak. We forget that when we breathe, we breathe in some original silence that preserves our relation to a life we forgot we're still living. That breath gains its greatest philosophical weight in the idea of the medieval *pneuma*; it is a breath we still breathe. The pneuma is, as Agamben writes of it, "the breath that animates the universe, [it] circulates in the arteries, and fertilizes the sperm [and] is the same one that, in the brain and in the heart, receives forms and phantasms of the things we see, imagine, dream, and love."[15] This breath connects the outermost limits of the world to the innermost excess of proximity, threads together the macrocosm and the microcosm, universe and self. That spirit substance that makes the star shine is the very same spirit substance that makes the sperm potent, that enlivens the heart with the images that dwell there. Medical knowledge of the time thought that the veins carried blood but that the arteries carried pneuma. Circulating through the entire body is this breath of the stars, this world breath. The pneuma connects and keeps livid the uncertain realm where the corporeal and the incorporeal join, maintains through their opposition an unforeseeable unity. The poem is a star chamber and a self-chamber through which the same breath blows.

I listen spheres of stars
I draw you close ever so
Communion come down and down
Quiet place to stop here
Who knows ever no one knows
to know unlove no forgive

Half thought thought otherwise
loveless and sleepless the sea
Where you are and where I would be
half thought thought otherwise
Loveless and sleepless the sea[16]

What does the poem do? It learns to listen to the stars, not to know, not to know. How does it learn not to know? How does it learn to listen?

The poem learns to breathe.

Body

Reductive, but maybe helpful, perhaps even honest, to say that Howe's poetry over the entire course of her books contain within them a continuous pivot that turning to one side opens onto poems whose nature explores the *pneumatic* line's spiritual implications and, turning to the other side, opens to a language whose nature explores the physical, the body of the voice or the voice as body. In part, this complexity in her work—work of spirit and work of body—arises as both a natural and an ethical consequence of the poetic ground she finds herself standing on: "I thought I stood on the shores of a history of the world where forms of wildness brought up by memory become desire and multiply."[17] Here the wilderness wilds itself, emerging from history's strict fact and wilding fact back into complexity, into desire, back into those bodies whose only evidence lurks within the "damaged edition's semi-decay" in which Howe finds her fertile soil. Like Oppen's deer in "Psalm," as she finds voices that are themselves bodies, the startle is that "they are there," roots dangling from their mouths, "scattering earth in the strange woods." It is here, in this location all the more real for needing imagination to find it, that Howe discovers the necessity for her radical vacillation between body and breath:

domain of transcendental subjectivity
Etymology the this

present in the past now
So many thread[18]

A "transcendental subjectivity" finds itself no longer limited to the self and the self's experience; rather, this self when it says "I" finds this pronoun of greatest intimacy, this word of the self-same, open on every side rather than closed. The "transcendental subject" finds herself apprehensive as a basic condition: fearful, yes, but also grasping, also seeking, also understanding. Words contain a history that includes us and exceeds us. A word points back through itself past the definite article to the accusative this (*Etymology* here ambivalent in such a way that it acts almost as a verb—almost as a verb in the imperative). *This* says we are in the presence of what has arrived from out of the past's wilds, shuttles the opened self into the past whose nature isn't history's index but now's experience. A word is a thread. The poem is a test of the words that fill it, a test that seeks to discover if the thread is strong enough to pull into itself that wilderness to which the poem is attached or strong enough for the poet herself to be pulled through the poem into that wilderness. Haunted, haunting work.

Howe seeks a way "To write against the ghost."[19] Such writing doesn't seek to negate but, by pressing against, to bring by the work of language in the crucible of poetic fervor the ghost into relief—as if the statue could step bodily out of the blank stone, or as a child rubs a crayon against the page until in every detail, down to the very veins, the leaf beneath appears.

The last, short section of *Souls of the Labadie Tract*, "Fragment of the Wedding Dress of Sarah Pierpont Edwards," re-materializes the body of the poem in a book remarkable in part for the pneumatic quality of the long series that precedes it. The first poem is the fragment of wedding dress itself, reproduced in black and white, a square cloth whose selvage on each side slightly frays, a partial blossom darker than the background cloth, one thread on the top arching above the whole like a solar flare. The fragment is as much a poem as the poem to follow—not simply an artifact for proof, not merely an evidence. Looking at it one feels that the fragment could be pulled apart thread by thread from any side of the fabric; likewise, one feels that from every margin threads could gather and weave themselves into the entire dress.

The fragment is a haunted intimacy—fragment of wedding dress and fragment of poem. The fabric points back to the body that wore it. Though the dress fragment appears flat, it has an inside that pressed against the body of Sarah Pierpont Edwards, and it has an outside that faces the world. To look at the square swatch of cloth long enough is to realize that one doesn't know which side of the fabric is seen—am I outside the body or am I within it? The poem fragment shares the same dilemma. The poems in the section feel comprised of a language pulled from multiple sources: definitions, descriptions both archival and speculative, personal notes, notational marginalia, historical facts, categorical ephemera. It is a language found and language assembled and a language created; it is a language frayed, a selvage language, a language marking the weave of its own construction, marking the schisms of its own damage. Certain lines are revelatory without being revealing:

the space of time into paper. Generation to[20]

And later:

fragile security   .   when alphabetic characters still
light of twighlight [sic] share the approaching sun
carrying traces[21]

The collage work emphasizes not only a pulling from multiple sources, or from differing registers of voice, but the helpless recognition that no voice is singular in its unity. Like some unconscious, inevitable Philomela, we speak by weaving a cloth that depicts our history—except our history is never merely our own. We seldom see how a line of poetry is simultaneously a vocalized reality and a tangible thread. Less often do we see that the threads with which we weave our voices are not a self-made material. The "alphabetic characters" carry traces. Those traces in part are the indefinite permutations of every use the alphabetic characters have been put to, as if words built of these letters contain in them those experiences that before our own lives they have named. We speak other lives when we speak our own—it is not enough to say we speak *of* them. We speak them. In Howe's poem there are these traces exerting themselves bodily in word as a material, in the word as fragment, in the fragment of the dress, in the dress's material. These fragments contain within themselves not only traces of history ongoing and so not history at all—Faulkner's "The past isn't dead. It's not even past"—but also contain within themselves the "twighlight" of the "approaching sun," that light that turns the material semi-transparent, that reveals behind the fragment, be it cloth or be it poem, the presence of the body or the absence of the body.

More to the difficult point, we find in the fragment itself the intimate definition of the poet's nature. Wordsworth's sense that the poet possesses "a disposition to be affected more than other men by absent things as if they were present" finds both confirmation and complication in Howe's work.[22] Howe's poems *present* absence, and *absent* presence. They make of themselves a fragment of the wedding dress turning itself always inside out and then outside in, confusing intimacy with surface, confounding surface with intimacy. Her work is a deeply erotic work, so the fragment of wedding dress is a fitting emblem to the nature not of the poet necessarily but of the poetry itself. The poem is both the external evidence of an internal work, as the thought moves into voice and voice exits the body into the vibrating air. But there is air inside the poem's body—breath, *pnuema*—also vibrating. The miraculous pivot in Howe's poetry is an exchange of breath because it is an exchange of body. We find ourselves within and without at once—wearing the dress we are admiring on the bride, inside the poem we are holding as we read it.

Affirming of Wordsworth's sense of the poet and poetry's work at one level, Howe also refutes him at another. Far from Wordsworth's "egotistical sublime" (cf. Keats's letter to Richard Woodhouse, October 27, 1818), Howe presents the apprehensive self, the open self, the adhesive self, and the permeable self. In *Singularities* she quotes from Deleuze and Guattari:

> The proper name (*nom propre*) does not designate an individual: it is on the contrary when the individual opens up to the multiplicities pervading him or her, at the outcome of the most severe operation of deperson-

alization, that he or she acquires his or her true proper name. The proper name is the instantaneous apprehension of a multiplicity. The proper name is the subject of a pure infinitive comprehended as such in a field of intensity.[23]

The voices gather in the name of the poet and give her her name. She is a body for their breath, and then also her breath fills their body. Who isn't a many and a one? Who isn't a ghosted chorus? Who isn't a body filled with breath?—or is it a breath filled with body?

Here the poem is the poet.
Here the poet haunts the haunted ground.
"Speak to me," Sappho says.
"Let me in" is a question and an answer.

Ghosts

Howe's poems alternate between materiality and intangibility; they never mark the line that divides their own opposition. We find instead poems built of languages found, gathered, and gleaned that Howe assembles into collages of intimate damage. These poems hover in some uncertain realm between clarity and dispersal, unable to signal within themselves a tendency toward manifestation or decay. Reading such poems, we feel witness to the holy moment when being decides to step into itself and begin to speak. But there are traces that remind one that in the midst of this bodying forth from *saying* to *said*, the construction is a wary one, finding in itself, on itself, those marks that map the intent of the construction, and so map the fault lines by which it may also fall apart. The majority of the poems in *That This*—Howe's most recent book, whose cover is the slate blue fragment of Sarah Pierpont Edward's wedding dress glimpsed in ghostly black and white in *Souls of the Labadie Tract*—show the spectral lines of the "invisible" tape holding these voices together. Those traces point back at the poet, whose adhesive effort leaves a ghostly demarcation. It cannot be helped. The poet ghosts the ghosts.

Conversely, we find poems (as in the majority of poems in *Souls of the Labadie Tract*) whose standard lineation offers only the most basic clue that in them an alternate (read altering; read alterity) work is occurring.

The differences are more profound, more mysterious. Here, too, voices arrive manifold but bear no mark of that multiplicity. Among those voices is Howe's own. It does not designate itself simply by saying *I*. Nor do the other voices name themselves nor offer their voices up for naming. To do so would be to commit a violence from which the poem itself might not recover—false claim of identity, of naming names, of pinning voice to history as a butterfly is pinned to a mat. Howe's effort opposes such reductions, resists such categorizations. Rather, the ethical effort infusing the poems must be reflected in the reader's ethical effort in experiencing the work. We must learn to read so others' voices may dwell in another voice; we must learn to read so as other voices may dwell in us. We must learn to hear the haunting chorus, that when we say *I* we say *I* for all.

A haunted voice denies that its primary value is historical. It speaks through itself not merely of the fact of its own occurrence but of that ongoing source that speaks through the fecund decay of the nearly forgotten words that populate and wild Howe's poems. That ongoing source could be called *origin*. It could be thought of as before history, as before language. It is precisely here—though "here" in Howe is no precise point—where the historical arrives not as any end in itself, not as any reclamation or revision or recovery, but arrives so as to open within itself another threshold, ontological in nature. History enters into the poem's realm not as a door closing or a wall fitting into place but enters with a casement window faultily latched in the midst of its certainty, half open in the midst of its facts. Yet, one must not forget that such openings, ontological in nature, are also violent. They have in them the violence of that which, once open, refuses to close.

We should also see, as Giorgio Agamben encourages,[24] that such violence marks the work of the poem concerned with tradition. Howe's poems radically redefine the nature of the traditional lyric. Ghosts demonize tradition's old dilemmas. They wander through the woods, these sourceless sources. They make the leaves shake. Howe invites them in, not merely into the content of her own poems but into her voice that opens on the page that metaphysical space the poem must first open within itself. The blank page is the place on which the poem is printed, but within the poem is another space, the haunted realm that occurs only after the words have been written:

Unconscious demarcations range

I pick my compass to pieces

Dark here in the drifting
In the spaces of drifting

Complicity battling redemption[25]

The traditional voice—that is, the voice that invites into it what is haunted by it—disorients itself through its own method. It creates the dark space of its own drifting. It realizes it is complicit in the creation of the very condition from which it wants to redeem those it discovers. Those voices:

Oh I see—I have to see
you fresh as those rough
streams are as power is

Caught—and wide awake

Oh—we are past saving
Aren't odd books full of us
What do you wake us for[26]

The voices themselves, "saved" into the poet's poems, ask why it is they're being awakened. (When such ghosts awake, they open their mouths and not their eyes.) To see "you fresh as those rough / streams" is to understand that the poem on the page cannot remove itself from a consideration of the history that precedes it. Such a poem doesn't venerate history but damages it, or is willing to damage it—damage, perhaps, to destruction complete. The traditional poem asks a question of which tradition is not the answer sought but, rather, that origin before tradition, underneath tradition. There is in the poem the furious effort to become its own source.

The genuinely traditional poem, of which in my mind Howe's is the necessary example, cannot take for granted the means by which it has come to its knowing but must pull up its own roots, must tear up and tear apart the very history that makes its own utterance possible. It must disturb its own roots. It is no simple act of reclamation. Nor is the effort to restore, to repair. It also disturbs the root that is the poet herself:

"Here we are"—You can't
hear us without having to be
us knowing everything we

know—you know you can't

Verbal echoes so many ghosts
poets I think of you as wild
and fugitive—"Stop awhile"[27]

The poet invites the ghosts into the poem and in doing so makes of the ghosts poets. The poem becomes some dwelling the poet writes so as to enter and in entering becomes less real, less than real, the countermotion of which is the arrival of the ghosts into the same space, an arrival that makes more real, more than real. Then their wildness finds confine; then they are not fugitive. But this poetry does not seek to tame. The nature of the confine is the poetic line that in uttering itself opens itself. In opening itself it opens to the utterances of the ghosts that fill it; the poet's line loses the narrow subjectivity of identity and grows multiple: "The tone of an oldest voice / Still one of great multitude."

Howe's work concerns the epistemological repercussions and the ethical consequences of the poem as a realm of gathering proximity. The voice gathers these ghosts; these ghosts gather in a voice. Milton's "darkness visible" seems too legible a construction to speak honestly about how the reader encounters the multiplicity of voices speaking within one another, and against one another, in Howe's poems. But Levinas's sense of the work of art existing in a "dark light" brings us closer to that light in which we might approach Howe's work—approach, as the poems themselves demand, so as to enter ourselves into that shade among the shades.

I keep you here to keep
your promise all that you
think I've wrought what

I see or do in the twilight
of time but keep forgetting
you keep coming back[28]

These ghosts, this multiple you, this other that is always others, this one that is always plural, keep entering into the twilit space of forgetting. These ghosts exist in the very space in which they cease to exist, they find remembrance in these very woods—"Language a wood for thought"[29]— where the non-experiential existing always within experience exerts ceaselessly its paradoxical condition.

This "dark light" illuminates its own obstructions. It alters radically the assumption a reader has toward a poem's own impetus toward formal completion. In these poems, where "Memory was and will be,"[30] incompletion replaces completion as the poem's end. All that exists within the unfinished, unfinishable limits of the poem's utterance—subject and object, speaker and spoken—finds itself fated to incompletion, an uncertain condition, half-lit or dark-lit, in which the poem's ethical complexity finds its difficult, stuttering expression. This ethical stuttering does not belong to the poet, for who now is the poet? Nor does it belong to the ghosts, for who are they? In the dark light of the poem, such distinctions can only be falsifications. It occurs in rhythm more than image, as Levinas writes, where rhythm

> represents a unique situation where we cannot speak of consent, assumption, initiative or freedom, because the subject is caught up and carried away by it. . . . It is so not even despite itself, for in the rhythm there is no longer a oneself, but rather a sort of passage from oneself to anonymity.[31]

Howe's willingness to write so as to create on the page that uncertain realm in which the ongoing work of radical proximity may continue marks not only the greatness of her project but also its most profound, and most complicated, ethical work. She writes so as to sentence herself to an anonymity that cannot be maintained, slipping back always into the narrow realm of singular self, but doing so in such a way that the traces of that "oldest voice of greatest multitude" require (more than merely make possible) the next poem into whose wilderness she casts her voice so as to open her voice and opens her voice so as to enter it just as others enter it. Just as we enter it who read her poems. The ethical work isn't one of clarification but one of mystification. Beyond even the Levinasian framework, in which the ethical obligation begins in the discovery of the supervening precedence of the other's face, we find in these bewildered poems a condition in which the face of the other cannot wholly be seen.

The face can't be seen, but the voice can be heard.

That voice is no single voice—though within it, as of the hiss at the universe's edge, one can hear, or imagine one hears, that pre-original, pre-language drone that marks the inexperiential edge where chaos hedges into cosmos. One can almost sense the limit, the binding source. But it is heard only by suffering this poetry's ethical difficulty, suffering it just as the poem suffers it:

Is one mind put into another
in us unknown to ourselves
by going about among trees
and fields in moonlight or in
a garden to ease distance to
fetch home spiritual things[32]

Perhaps there is no other home than the home poetry offers, the home the poem is. Open the door to that home and find the wilderness growing in it. The poem contains the forest it wanders through, continual mystical inversion of form and content. The poem contains what contains it. Is it that one writes so as to enter? A word being a door and a wood and a wild leaf and an initiation? To enter is to find in one's own mind another mind, many minds, each with a mind in its own. Confounded among the trees, in the moonlit fields. The effort, as the poem so plainly says, is to "ease distance to / fetch home spiritual things." Such things are ghosts, are phantasms, these images-not-quite-images that invoke in the singular subject that ethereal obligation to dismantle the edifice of one's merest self, ego's iota, and to let the ghosts climb into the poem, dwell in the voice, multiply and sing, accuse and comfort, and make of the poet's mouth only a crooked path in a dark forest, whose trees branch up through the brain, whose leaves open not to the sun but to this dark light, the word's own shining, call it responsibility, and whose echo from the edges calls back, *response.*

Thinking as Burial Practice

Exhuming a Poetic Epistemology in Thoreau, Dickinson, and Emerson

I think a lot about thinking—it never gets me too far. I don't know why I expect it to be different. I have this feeling that I should be getting somewhere, but mostly I find myself still sitting in the same chair, holding the same book, wondering at which word it was where I stopped reading, even while looking at the page, even while wondering what a poem is, what thinking in a poem looks like, how it feels to think, even while wondering why it is once again I have these images in my head of the spiraled, bent-down grass where the deer bedded for the night, and then the deer with the roots of the grass in her mouth, the dirt falling back to the ground while she chews. I consider digestion, breath, heartbeat, these processes of the body governed not by mind but by genius in the oldest sense, that daemonized life that ensures our own life continue, lest in not remembering to breathe we cease to do so, and so of the heart, and so of the gut, these vitalities that require we forget them for them to go on; and in forgetting them, our minds are afforded some other kind of work. Maybe it's thinking. I think about appetite. I consider that between mouth and anus there is a single corridor that is a form of absence, and we live by filling this absence with things we eat, we organize ourselves around what is missing and keep trying to fill it with world, though the world passes right through. What is the story of Eden but an ongoing reminder that to know we must take a bite and swallow? And what is this paradise of and in the mind, those digestive circuits that take in through the eyes a poem or a book and the essence feeds some occult muscle and what is cast back out is but another poem, written, perhaps, by my own hand, or a sentence, perhaps, written by your own? I wonder about the mind as the thing that is missing. And I wonder what it feels like to think and if I have ever felt that thing called thinking. I wonder if I've ever done it: thinking. I worry it feels like sitting in a chair, realizing I've become blind to the page I'd been reading, and so once again I must begin to read the poem I'd started earlier—maybe a minute ago, maybe yesterday, I can't quite remember, that poem I began, and when I did so, maybe when I opened my eyes and took a first breath and cried. I worry a paragraph is a cloud waiting to disperse. I worry about the blank page, if it's a field, and, if so, what type? Field of oblivion, apophatic ground, terrifying "there is" of pure being. Or is it just the pale grasses all pressed down after the living thought has wandered gently off to graze?

Forgive this confused reverie, or should I say, this reverie of confusion. I mean to ask a simple question. Which direction does thinking go in? I know that question has in it some naïve assumption the postmodern world easily dismisses: linearity as false vector, hubris of teleology, and so on. I'm all for the multivalent complexity of thought, but can't it be— that as "a point is that which has no part," and a line "a breadth of endless length" made up of points that have no parts—that thinking can move within itself with all its adhesive valencies and still be in motion in one direction or another? Up or down or to the horizon? At the same time, I feel so distrustful of ideal form, of Plato's "divided line," of his cave, of *Eidos*, of the Forms, of the soul as horse-drawn chariot—well, I distrust them even as I love them all the more for my doubt. I want to know why it might be that when I try to think, I don't find myself in airless realms where truth's cold pastoral holds desire at bay so the ideal form can hold sway over the soul; I want to know why my hands are dirty. I want to know how I got this dried mud in my eye. I want to know who dug this hole I'm standing in, right now, while I sit reading in this chair.

It is this sense of direction, of thoughtful momentum, that I want to consider by turning to three touchstones of my own mental life—and if of mine, so perhaps of your own. Each is very brief, but as Thomas Traherne suggests that a single leaf is worth a century of meditation, and Blake suggests heaven is there in the wildflower, each may require more thought than the life doing the thinking can provide. A sentence in Thoreau, a sentence or two in Emerson, and one poem from Dickinson—just these, no more.

• • •

In the second chapter of *Walden*, "Where I lived, and What I lived For," Thoreau writes, "My instinct tells me that my head is an organ for burrowing, as some creatures use their snout and fore-paws, and with it I would mine and burrow my way through these hills."[1] I trust this creaturely turn, this synecdoche in which head stands in for that organ mind, and whatever thinking is, it digs more than it soars. "To mine" and "to burrow" replace more typical images of the mental process. One seeks the "richest vein" coursing within the hills; the other knows that dwelling is the effort of deepest thinking. No longer is thought a means by which one is removed from the stuff of the world up into those ethereal realms where Forms replace matter with a pattern more primary if less tangible. No. Thinking is to dig down into the matter itself, to give over to the old occult sense that only within things can their truest worth be found—vein evocative not only of gold and silver and diamond but also of blood, also of the earth-thing that is the body. In seeking that which is of known worth, valued by society, by world, one creates that space that none can value as highly as the one who has formed it, this burrow that none can exactly borrow, this work of thinking so as to make a place to dwell not *on* the world but *in* it, to become an indweller. So quietly, but so audaciously, Thoreau offers us a means by which to revalue work we assume we know the purpose and worth of. Thinking leads to knowledge, that rich vein, common sense claims. But for those of us who, like Thoreau, find our sense anathema to common sense, thinking's relation to the knowledge it is supposed to find turns paradoxical. One doesn't gain knowledge; one created in it a hole, and in that hole one learns how to live. To have that instinct that your head is an organ for burrowing is likewise to trust that it is a tool dependent on ignorant uses as much as it is for thoughtful ones. To shovel out this hole with my head is as good a use of it as discovering the Pythagorean theorem. It takes the otherworldly work of mind and makes it into under-worldly work. Within the solid hill, within the dark ground, within the solid fact, we think so as to open a space to breathe, make inside of something some nothing in which we can take a breath, go to sleep, and wake. To wake up we must dig down. Thoreau writes:

> To be awake is to be alive. I have never yet met a man who was quite
> awake. How could I have looked him in the face?
>
> We must learn to reawaken and keep ourselves awake, not by mechan-
> ical aids, but by the infinite expectation of the dawn, which does not for-
> sake us in our soundest sleep.[2]

That "soundest sleep" that the "infinite expectation of dawn" doesn't for-
sake isn't merely untroubled. That *sound* also invokes itself as a verb, as a
whale sounds when it dives to the ocean's bed, suggesting sleep as a quality of depth, a going into, a going under the mountain to be within the
vein. The sleep that occurs is not the sleep of knowledge, sufficient unto
itself, but rather the sleep within knowledge, that forgetfulness at the
center of fact, that *lethe* in the heart of *aletheia*, which orients us back to
the expectation of the dawn not as the beginning of just another day but
that ongoing first morning, heroic in its gold light, a morning not of time
but of condition, in which we wake to wonder that the world is a form of
ongoingness that breaks the husk of our intellect back to the germ of first
consciousness. How do we find the dawn? We crawl back out of the hole
we dug. Shake the dirt from our ears. Open our eyes.

· · ·

"Morning is when I am awake and there is dawn in me," Thoreau says.[3] To
wake in it is to be awakened "by our Genius." I love the plural possessive
pronoun he uses—not *my*, but *our*. As no one owns the morning, so no
one possesses genius. Some other quality lurks. It is almost as if, heard
properly, there is a passive quality to such possession, to such genius. One
doesn't master so much as be mastered; doesn't possess so much as finds
oneself possessed. To crawl out of the burrow head first means one opens
one's eyes to a dawn that fills the head with its light, and for the briefest of instants, the mind blinded by the sudden clarity as an eye might
be blinded by lightning, dawn occurs within even as it occurs without,
internal and external lose their opposition, and thinking begins not by
collecting once again the already-thought thoughts but by finding the
categories of consideration obliterated by the light they meant to record.
That fecund zero might be one way to describe genius, mimetic as it is of
the eye opened widest, of the mouth saying its invocatory reflex, O.

But do we crawl out of Thoreau's burrow beneath the hills carrying only that capacity for nothingness that lets us possess the dawn by being possessed by it, or is there something else, something we bring, something mined from that "richest vein" beneath the hill?

In "The Poet" Emerson writes, "Every word was once a poem. Every new relation is a new word."[4] And in the same essay, "Language is fossil poetry."[5] Whatever the instinct to dig with our heads might mean, suffice it to say that the mining at which it works isn't after gold or silver merely material in nature, though seeking it outside of the world in which it is embedded is a sophisticated craft—one that would point at the hill and say there is the gold, which no doubt is true, but falls short of the dirt of experience. But gold and silver are a kind of fossil, as are diamonds, as are gems. Not the fossils of the textbooks that show the bones of the beasts now extinct, a kind of proof that a life has been without the possibility of a return to the same, but these richest veins of ore are fossils of those volcanic processes whose heat and pressure like some furious genius heaved the world into being and in doing so created a vascular system coursing through mountains and hills and earth. They are evidence of a processes still occurring, where elemental forces work on the elements themselves, cosmic law grown material, as vital in the hill as is the vein of blood in the wrist, and evidence of the same principle, that volcanic heart yoking to its pressure the volcanic head that thinks only by virtue of the veins pulsing their particulate gold within it.

We emerge, if we do, if we ever begin digging in the first place, not only with that nothing of the radically open eye but with a fossil. We carry it in us until it becomes molten once again; we carry it with us until it becomes alive. It is maybe no more than a word but a word of different nature than those that tend to fill the days that merely go away. It is a word with a burrow inside it, a word that invites the thing it names into it to exist, to live, just as the thing it names reciprocates the kindness and finds within its substance some absence for the word to take up its lodging. I suspect this is in part what Emerson means when he claims that "every new relation is a new word." It's not a word made up; it's no neologism. It's a word tuned back to its initial life, its morning life, its life made purely of dawn, wherein what it names it names for the first time, not recognition but initiatory experience, the very atom of intelligence before the mind falls into the trap of its own consciousness and confuses thinking with being.

But it begins underground, this work. And it's hard to know what and where the ground is. It looks like there's sky all around. It's hard to know how to use the head as your shovel. It's difficult to guess that some of the soil is blue.

· · ·

Even the briefest encounter with Emily Dickinson's poetry reveals a mind uniquely indebted to the grave. Easy enough to call the tendency macabre or gothic in sensibility, but to do so would undermine an epistemological experiment that extends far past death as subject matter or obsession and instead insists that death, and thinking, and expression, and sense, must be seen to weave one into the other. This graveyard work (and as I write these sentences, sitting outside, the mourning dove complains her song) abounds in the lyric imagination of America: "I heard a Fly buzz—when I died—"; "I cannot live with You— / It would be life— / And Life is over there—"; "I am nobody! Who are you?"; "Because I could not stop for death— / he kindly stopped for me—"; and "A Death blow is a Life blow to Some" are only a fraction of well-known and lesser so examples. It is this sense of some vitality that begins at death—that experience Wittgenstein reminds us "is not an event of life"—that most concerns me.[6] Death would seem to be both the border and the border guard simultaneously, the line that marks sense from silence and the one who, in allowing you to cross, warns there is no crossing back. That limit we find ourselves at, some limit we might call our life, filled with the experiences by which we lived it, seems suddenly not to be the resource we thought it was, some means by which to feel we've gained an identity that is unique to our own peculiar bliss—but then bliss meets abyss, and what had felt complete stands suddenly apart, partial, and we find within ourselves something ajar, "just the Door ajar / That Oceans are— and Prayer—."[7]

How to be upon that ocean, to be within it; or, to stick closer to our overriding metaphor, how to be within the earth, in the burrow, where the localities and precisions of *topos* are denied us, where we live within being lost, becomes our dearest poetic question. Dickinson's poem 280 might go some way toward illuminating the void that death is supposed to be:

I felt a Funeral, in my Brain,
And Mourners to and fro
Kept treading—treading—till it seemed
That Sense was breaking through—

And when they all were seated,
A Service, like a Drum—
Kept beating—beating—till I thought
My Mind was going numb—

And then I heard them lift a Box
And creak across my Soul
With those same Boots of Lead, again,
Then Space—began to toll,

As all the Heavens were a Bell,
And Being, but an Ear,
And I, and Silence, some strange Race
Wrecked, solitary, here—

And then a Plank in Reason, broke,
And I dropped down, and down—
And hit a World, at every plunge,
And Finished knowing—then—[8]

The first two quatrains contain a curious paradox: they speak of feeling emerging as a consequence of the end of the faculty by which we think we recognize feeling—that is, the end of thought. In some lovely echo of Keats's "drowsy numbness" that "pains my heart," Dickinson feels the same numbness in her mind, a strange cessation of that inner noise we call thinking and the language in which it occurs, perverse work of consciousness that grows aware by growing apart from the object of its attention, and the ear that for a lifetime secretly became trained almost wholly inward—solipsism of *I think, therefore I am* ad nauseum, ad infinitum—reverses its listening and tunes once again to the world outside the head.

The inversion of the ear back to an orientation geared wholly outside of the self not only allows the soul to become a force in the poem—that silence apart from all speaking even as it is within all word, burrowed there, vein of purest nothing—it also allows the ear to become *supra-sensory*, hearing not a single song, but that resonance that, as from a struck bell, reverberates through all being as a grace note. Here, that bell is heaven—not God's dwelling place, not religious dogma, but that next sphere of cosmic order whose own ringing is but a listening to the celestial sphere also encircling it.

One might say the brain is simply a bell without a tongue; we must learn to be quiet to let it ring. And so it is that Dickinson finds herself next to silence, both "wrecked," both "solitary," both "here." That silence may well be the chaos of old, waiting for a motion it cannot produce itself to spring from it that deepest possibility of this form of order we call life. It cannot act upon itself; it must be acted upon. And it is just there, on that ground more justly called an abyss, the self-wreck of being and silence, that mere plank of a nothing-that-is, barest board of reason, where the burying work of real thinking begins. It does not feel like thinking. It feels like a plunge, like a plummet. In that downward motion alone is the world found, are worlds found, and to "finish knowing—then—," is not to end in fact or wisdom; it is to be reborn into an utmost ignorance, an absolute infancy, where knowing as an end of thinking is over, just as the fairy tales that put children to sleep all come to an end. That little death called sleep is also an introduction to our mental life. But sometimes one has to die in more deliberate ways. Sometime you use your own head to dig your own grave, and deep in the earth, looking for fossils, you learn how to listen. "Every word was once a poem." And right there, where knowing ends, something else begins. You might call it thinking.

"The Oracular Tree Acquiring"

On Romanticism as Radical Practice

I. A First Glance, through the Ear; or, Music as Vermifuge

In September 1851 Henry David Thoreau returned repeatedly to "the new telegraph wire" to hear the music in the air. The music sang not only in the air, though the wind blowing across the tense wires gave the "sound of a far-off glorious life, a supernal life" that "vibrated in the lattice-work of this life of ours"; the music also resonated in the poles holding the wires up. Then,

> I put my ear to one of the posts, and it seemed to me as if every pore of the wood was filled with music, labored with the strain—as if every fibre was affected and being seasoned or timed, rearranged according to a new and more harmonious law. Every swell and change or inflection of tone pervaded and seemed to proceed from the wood, the divine tree or wood, as if its very substance was transmuted. What a recipe for preserving wood, perchance—to keep it from rotting—to fill its pores with music![1]

Thoreau hears inside the vibrating wood the accumulating "prophetic fury"—a prophecy not of words, nor in words, but a harmonious rage whose meaning eludes interpretation. One cannot know if one is damned or saved, being forewarned or being welcomed into the next new world—there is only the fact of the perception itself, a hearing that is also a feeling, and the thoughts born there that find no cure in knowing.

These passages in which Thoreau hears the music "working terribly within" the wood have vibrated themselves into the latticework of my own life.* I have come to think of them not as a Romantic principle (perhaps there is in Romanticism no such thing as a "principle") but as a Romantic realization. The telegraph wires strung tightly between poles carry human words across distances over which the spoken voice of its own power could not cross. The wires carry the words instantly. But it is not those words that create this music, this music that both thrills Thoreau and seems in ways to terrify him. What carries the words makes the music possible, the wires themselves. Here, the Aeolian harp of Romantic fancy takes on a far more startling dimension, in which the wire of our own voices is that against which the "supernal" music must blow to be heard. One might extend the thought in its astonishing trajectory—that the meaning in the human voice, the meaning strung not only along the telegraph wires but also those wires that are the lines of a poem, has very little to do with what the spoken or written words mean and everything

---

*Latticework is deeply significant as an image for my experience of how Romanticism has affected my own poetic practice. A lattice is formed of a grid and so can be thought of as a kind of matrix. Here the opposed interweaving slats that make up the lattice provide a symbol in which, say, the opposed notions of theory and practice are interwoven into a structure whose very integrity depends on the inability to tell one apart from the other. Romanticism, for my own poetic efforts, has undone the ability to give precedence to either theory or practice but, instead, has shown that the deep formal life of a poem invests itself in confounding easy notions of causality and consequence—a confusion so profound that to pull one slat from the other results in the collapse of the whole structure. Just as important to me, though, and found only by taking Romanticism's encouragement toward the poem as a form of experience in and of itself, is the thought that such a lattice has another, more important purpose than simply providing for its structural integrity. It also serves as a form upon which the creeping vines grow, gives a formal life to that which must climb another structure in order to live. It does feel to me that to write a poem is to create just such a lattice—a work that must be concerned with its own formal life in the absurd hope that it will allow another life to continue to grow, an organic one, a flower-life, which, when flourishing, makes of the lattice itself a plant. This sense I have of my own poems being not simply a form and a life of their own but one deeply in service to those previous works that fill tradition— these works I love and in whose care I tend to see my own writing—has led me to increasingly find ways to interweave my own words with the words of others, to make a lattice of them, an interwoven structure but a structure that is itself alive—as sometimes, as I've seen I in my garden, the pea plants twine around themselves to rise. *This Nest, Swift Passerine* (Tupelo, 2009) is perhaps my most radical experiment in such Romantic hopes.

to do with creating in every line a tension that allows the unheard breeze blowing over the surface of all things (page and world and mind teetering between both) to gain sensibility, to thrill into harmony. "The fibres of all things have their tension, and are strained like the strings of lyre."

I cannot help but hear, in the tense lyre string of my own mind, Keats's lines, "but here there is no light, / save what from heaven is with the breezes blown,"[2] in which the wind carries light from an upper realm to a lower realm, a light that is not wholly light, interweaving the latticework of one world into that of another, claiming inside music, vision. In complete darkness, the nightingale singing ever farther away, Keats names every flower whose scent he can smell, brought to him on this heaven-blown breeze. This is not a vision *of* but a vision *in*. As with Thoreau's "telegraph harp," Keats's perception creates itself out of a synesthesia, which, rather than one sense evoking the work of another, might here be best understood as perception itself becoming perceptive; Romantic realization erupts out of crisis, that unexpected moment when the conditions of daily life unfold into vaster possibilities. Then it is not enough for the eye to see nor the nose to smell nor the ear to listen. Then the senses themselves must sense, must rely on powers not simply their own: the ear learns to see, the eye to listen. Deep inside Romantic urgency resides the seemingly modern notion that the poem does not record experience but, rather, shows how experience experiences itself and does so not as an intellectual gesture but as a personal revelation. Here, too, the personal extends into the universal, is implicated intricately outside of itself. A link is formed. Thoreau hears the music he feels. Such music grants the eye not the object seen but the light by which the object may be seen. It is just such music that Thoreau sees when he listens, his ear against the wood, and learns that in all empty spaces, music vibrates, not simply occupying absence but entering absence so as to preserve what is otherwise riddled with holes, open to rot. It is music that preserves.

Thoreau's friend Ralph Waldo Emerson suggests a similar audacity: "Genius is the activity which repairs the decay of things."[3] Genius is an idea not yet abandoned in Romanticism but hearkened after in all its ancient oddity. Thoreau goes even further in his suggestion. That music playing itself on the telegraph harp? It is an ingenious music. If it vibrates in the pores of the wood, then it vibrates in the pores of the skin, in the lacunae of the bones—our skin and our bones. The work of writing creates in oneself a musical tension by which another music may be heard. We sing to hear that other singing which can only be heard within, or against, the music of our own voice. It is this genius that repairs us (this genius always imperfectly other) and repairs not only us but also repairs our relation to the world of which we sing.

To hear it is to be changed by it. When Thoreau puts his ear to the post and finds music in every gap, he also establishes a radical metonymy. The telegraph pole extends his ear, resonates not only with the music that fills it but simultaneously with the ability to perceive that music as well. It is a moment of profound imagination, as Coleridge writes it:

> They and they only can acquire the philosophical imagination, the sacred power of self-intuition, who within themselves can interpret and understand the symbol, that the wings of the air-sylph are forming within the skin of the caterpillar; those only, who feel in their own spirit the same instinct, which impels the chrysalis of the horned fly to leave room in its involucrum for antennæ yet to come.[4]

The telegraph pole—and the image of a man with a stripped tree springing out of his head almost absurd in its literalness—becomes Thoreau's antenna. Every object promises the same extension—not simply an extension of self but an expansion of the receptivity of the self to the world, whose spiritual instinct realizes the entire world is an ear horn and we but one of the half deaf who bring our ear next to the object to better hear the song.

Thoreau claims there is "no better vermifuge" than such vibrating music. It expels the worms that eat the wood. The tense lyre-string of my own mind cannot help but hear Blake:

O rose, Thou art sick!
The invisible worm
That flies in the night,
In the howling storm,

Has found out thy bed
Of crimson joy;
And his dark, secret love
Does thy life destroy.[5]

The same wind on which the worm flies blows across these lines. In them, the telegraph harp also sings. It is a terrible harmony that forces the worm to abandon his love. It is a music in our own fiber. It vibrates in us—if we can establish within ourselves the needed tension—and so removes from within us the worm. It also, more shockingly, reveals that in this rose world we are also the worm. It changes, this music, our own parasitic nature—this living off the world a kind of love that destroys the world. We care about what we kill. But that is not enough. Thoreau has found that musical vibration that alters our relationship to the world in which we live. It is a music that casts us out of ourselves. Do you hear it? Put your ear against the wood and listen. Put your ear against the page. Inside a voice is another voice, inside a song another song. Do you hear it?

It tells us to forget who we are.

II. "What shocks the virtuous philosopher, delights the camelion Poet"

In the telegraph pole of the letter *I*—a line that stands up from its slumber, a line perpendicular to the horizon—hides a labyrinth. When I say *I*, I speak this labyrinth. I am inside this *I* I speak, monster and sacrifice indistinguishable, monster and sacrifice both. One can think of the poem as Theseus's thread unspooling itself behind the hero's speculative wandering, but to envision the dilemma fully it must become fully impossible. This impossibility is not the complexity of the maze, this I who riddles itself with saying *I*. What is impossible is that the labyrinth cannot be seen save by the thread coursing through it, the line—these lines of the poem—by which means the maze is meant to be escaped. The line marks the maze, reveals its trap, illuminates (even if in half-light) the intricate riddle. The poem reveals the crisis we do not know we are in, difficult gift. It is a strange form of recognition that forsakes clarity for complexity— self revealed not as what one knows, not (as Keats has it, "my identical self") as a resource of subjective certainty, but as an uncertain quantity whose deepest necessity is being in motion. This labyrinth self is a self of self-abandonment: self cast into itself as its unforeseen, impossibly unforeseeable, crisis.

Wordsworth's in/famous definition of the poet's work can now begin to take on its more radical hue:

I have said that Poetry is the spontaneous overflow of powerful feelings: it takes its origin from emotion recollected in tranquility: the emotion is contemplated till by a species of reaction the tranquility gradually disappears, and an emotion, kindred to that which was before the subject of contemplation, is gradually produced, and does itself actually exist in the mind.[6]

A poem begins in a tranquility that its own work ends; it begins in an absence whose end is presence—but here no presence is pure. It is a presence complicated by the fact of itself. The poet places herself in this crisis of herself, a crisis the poem actualizes, conjures into a world, makes real even as it undermines its own reality. This labyrinth self, this riddle *I*, is a curious prologue to the difficulty of representation, in which the certainty of self is transformed into uncertainty so that the world can be real and simultaneously questionable in its reality. The mind wonders about that world through which it wanders. The poem must become the forest through which it marks a path; the poem must create the distance it crosses. This questionable world—so reminiscent of our postmodern condition that the cutting edge of contemporary thought reveals itself on an antique blade—places poetry, and so the *I* through which the poem comes to be, in a strange relation to world and knowledge.[**†] A poem is

---

[**†]It is within this crisis of self, this riddle of *I*, that Martin Corless-Smith's work gains one of its radically romantic valencies. Of any contemporary poet that comes quickly to mind, Corless-Smith is returning to the roots of the Romantic tradition—a poetic gesture not of exhumation, nor of the critic's effort to classify the previously living strand, but rather a method of digging down to the roots so as to revivify them, to show that the vitality never left, and to graft his own experiment onto this previous experiment whose organic life never ceased its living. (I think perhaps it is the poet who understands Thoreau's conviction that the "head is an organ for burrowing"; it is the poet who knows one doesn't graft the fruit of one limb to the differing fruit of another but grafts at the root and becomes the plant one is grafted to.) All of Corless-Smith's books prove relevant to this discussion, but his third book, *Nota* (Fence, 2003) is on my mind much these days. In it, the poet writes, "There are those, including often the self, who you cannot abide—but those, especially the self, that you must." Harsh wisdom. Wisdom that confronts and does not comfort. It also provides not a sentiment but a suspicion that Romantic work is anything but "romantic." That is, the work of encounter, of self in enveloping collision with other and with self, is in its erotic trouble dizzying, maddening, and labyrinthine as often (if not more often) than it is epiphanic. The

the fact beneath the fact, not a bedrock foundation but a seismic fault that is remarkably sensitive to the convective motion of molten center whose upheavals make possible the very land it shakes.

The mind, too, is a convective process. It is within such molten light that certain audacities of Romantic thought might be seen. Wordsworth's "Poetry is the first and last of all knowledge" bears relationship to Emerson's similarly volcanic (i.e., generative *and* apocalyptic) insight:

> For poetry was all written before time was, and whenever we are so finely organized that we can penetrate into that region where the air is music, we hear those primal warblings and attempt to write them down, but we lose ever and anon a word or a verse and substitute something of our own, and thus miswrite the poem.[7]

The initial claim in both quotes is one, as Keats might say, that would "shock the virtuous philosopher." Both Wordsworth and Emerson give to poetry a special being verging on impossible being. Poetry—here a general realm, a realm of genius, the genuine field—precedes the poem. Poetry is before and after the poem as much as it is "the first and last of all knowledge." Epistemologies want to explain the labyrinth in which they hide. Poetry exists before knowledge, before the experience that leads to knowledge, an impossible a priori in which experience occurs

---

poem, like the self, might be considered "a field where nothing borders nought," but as a field (location *and* practice) it is also a place of dwelling. In the midst of *Nota*, Corless-Smith places a book within a book: "A Selection from the Works of Thos. Swan (MS. 8911 Worcester City Records Office)." The inserted book purports to be a discovery of another poet's notebooks, filled with notes (on the odd nature of color, etc.) and poems in various states of vision/re-vision. The poems bear enough of a lyric sensibility that the reader suspects Corless-Smith is the poet who wrote them. But the perfection of his mask is its imperfection. For the poems, too, differ, and one suspects—even as one tries to dismiss—that Swan's poems are truly written by Swan himself. But what is it that "truly written" signifies? Our desire for "authority" proves itself to be a suspicious desire. That suspicion is Corless-Smith's Romantic inheritance—one that he admirably, necessarily furthers. It is a lyric ambivalence that also casts light back onto such proto-Moderns as Fernando Pessoa as profoundly Romantic in their experiment. Indeed, it might be heteronym as polytropic self, a self that never can unify into mere self—self as that indeterminate point in which accuracy and inaccuracy are interchangeable—that typifies radical romantic personhood.

before itself, a pattern akin to fate, but a fate always flawed by the self who receives its sentence. Romanticism claims poetry as that difficult art that shows us the condition we are in by making that amazed condition apparent. The cost of the gift is being included in the gift's trap, and to fail is to both escape the maze and to be lost in it. The drama inherent at the most fundamental level of poetic activity—that is, in the writing of a poem—exacerbates the fault line lurking between *I think* and *I am*. The poem calls into question not only experience but how experience is experienced. It calls into question the very experience it creates—an experience of itself, its own textual life, but a life never circumscribed by its own limits, by its own language. For the labyrinth of the poem, like the labyrinth of a nervous system, finely attunes itself to the possible existence of another—world or person, world that is a person, that other who is also real.

Emerson sees that the poet must be "finely organized" to penetrate into the poetry that precedes the poem. The poet is a pattern before she is a person. As Thoreau could hear the music filling the pores of the telegraph pole by virtue of being himself filled with holes (What are the senses but proof of our porousness?), so poetry takes advantage of what is world in us before it takes advantage of what in us is self. Before self-saying, before personality and talent, we might see ourselves as a smaller pattern (Donne: "I am a little world made cunningly") within the larger pattern of the world. These patterns seem different, create difference, and so create thought, create knowledge, whose authority thrives in creating hierarchy and category that difference itself reveals and makes possible. But poetry is before knowledge, is written before time; the poem contains the knowledge it creates (a faulty, fault-like construction); it occurs in the very time its eternal inclinations wish to repudiate. One might think of two glass discs each marked with a pattern, each rotating at its own speed, in its own direction, and to all observers the patterns are different, until both rotate in such a way that the patterns align and, through what had been a patterned opacity, pierces a sudden light—except it is us who are one of these discs. We are no outside observers. The world is the other disc. And when the patterns align, the light is not seen by us but moves through us, is not knowledge but revelation, is light falling *through* before it falls *upon*, light as that through which sight occurs, a seeing light, a light through which we see that we see.

But vision ends in or at an object—it is not possible to remain in light's transport, in its conveyance. Destination is destiny; consciousness, a step outside. Something is seen; someone sees it. It is a reductive definition, but perhaps a useful one, to say the poetic process perceives an exterior world the perception of which internalizes that world, that the mind in its amalgamation of memory and imagination recognizes that world and seeks a language by which to describe it. It is awfully simple, but maybe necessary, to say that the poem is that description. It is just as important to say, and perhaps more difficult, that the poem undermines the stability of the boundary that keeps self and world separate and simultaneously undoes the ease of its own definitive urge, defining world in order to torment that definition with doubt. Romanticism shows us that we do not doubt *what is not*, but must learn to doubt *what is*. The poet writes into existence an object—made of words and to what words fallibly refer—that claims existence for that reality that precedes the poem's own work. Witness is its own riddle that suspects it must create a world to say the world is real.

Just such amazed intricacy underlies the Romantic sense of poetry's impossible relation to knowledge and experience. Coleridge's sense of poetic wholeness that "reveals itself in the balance or reconcilement of opposite or discordant qualities" includes the illogical harmony in which the reality of the poem precedes its own manifestation of that reality. The poem sees that the past is ahead of it, the past is where it's going—a genuine fate in place of an ingenuous fact, in which every word's work is an attempt to reach back to that first moment of consciousness when word and world impossibly coexisted as one. Shelley hears the beauty of this dilemma when in his "Defence" he writes of the child singing who "seeks, by the prolonging in its voice and motions the duration of the effect, to prolong also a consciousness of the cause."[8] The poem, as does the child's song, sings in order to retrieve the world back into consciousness; it is also by the song's being sung the world is lost.

Recollection in tranquility begins in absence being made aware of itself. A perceptive nothing. The poet, let's say, is a nothing that sings. The song is a song of presence. The world is what is present. The song is not conscious of the world but presents the world to consciousness. When the singer ceases to sing, when the words are no longer in the air but on the page, when ink bears what breath once bore, then the mind reaches its mute terror—that its reality is excluded from the reality it knows. Emerson understands that we mar the music we hear by noting it down. That flawed pattern—it is ourselves.

It is me.

I am the place to be abandoned.

III. "not myself goes home to myself"

Language others us. John Keats, on October 27, 1818, wrote a famous letter in which he described this primary poetic difficulty:

> As to the poetical Character itself (I mean that sort of which, if I am any thing, I am a Member; that sort distinguished from the wordsworthian or egotistical sublime; which is a thing per se and stands alone) it is not itself—it has no self—it is every thing and nothing—It has no character—it enjoys light and shade; it lives in gusto, be it foul or fair, high or low, rich or poor, mean or elevated—It has as much delight in conceiving Iago as Imogen. What shocks the virtuous philosopher, delights the camelion Poet. It does no harm from its relish of the dark side of things more than from its taste for the bright one; because they both end in speculation. A Poet is the most unpoetical of any thing in existence; because he has no Identity—he is continually in for—and filling some other Body—The Sun, the Moon, the Sea and Men and Women who are creatures of impulse are poetical and have about them an unchangeable attribute—the poet has none; no identity—he is certainly the most unpoetical of God's Creatures. If then he has no self, and if I am a Poet, where is the Wonder that I should say I write no more? . . . It is a wretched thing to confess; but is a very fact that not one word I ever utter can be taken for granted as an opinion growing out of my identical nature—how can it, when I have no nature? When I am in a room with People if I ever am free from speculating on creations of my own brain, then not myself goes home to myself: but the identity of every one in the room begins so to press upon me that I am in a very little time annihilated—not only among Men; it would be the same in a Nursery of children.[9]

The postmodern poet has inherited a notion of the Romantic poet as one for whom world and self and other are easily and too sweetly amalgamated into a universal whole, a unity in which difference ceases to exert its pressing difficulty, where clouds throw down their shadows on hills of daffodils, but the weather will pass, and the sun shines equally on each and all. I fear it is our naiveté that accuses them of naiveté. I find in Keats's notion of the "Poetical character" a fearsomeness that predicts Rimbaud's imperative for the poet's deepest life: "But the soul has to be made monstrous, that's the point." But unlike Rimbaud—writing some sixty years after Keats wrote his letter to Richard Woodhouse—who claims that the "first study for a man who wants to be a poet is the knowledge of himself, complete," Keats bears no such notions of the poet possessing, nor needing to possess (nor being able to possess), a complete knowledge of the self. Romanticism places its poetic brunt at the very crisis where existence of world and self, and knowledge of world and self, are not determined but undetermined (even undermined) by the poet's work—expression, song—and the self is far from the certain container in which curious perceptions morph clearly into strange facts. For Keats, it is the self that is monstrous: "Might I not at that very instant have been cogitating on the Characters of Saturn and Ops?" Whereas Rimbaud suggests the soul must *become* monstrous, Keats sees that the soul's nature is monstrous, for its nature is not identical. The soul is the other. The soul contradicts simple notions of self, dispels easy notions of essence, for the soul—taken as a reality, a poetic reality—places a manifold and plural anonymity at the fundament of identity.

This sense of soul-self being manifold, porous, free-floating, rupturing, othering, closely replicates Wordsworth's and Emerson's impossible epistemology in which poetry precedes experience, precedes knowledge. Here, in Keats, we see, too, that self precedes self, person precedes personality, and the work of the poet is not to create in herself that which is unique but, far the opposite, to deconstruct what feels original merely because it strikes one as individual and, instead, to rid oneself of merest self in order to venture into what is in common. Language others us because language is what is in common.

Romanticism begins, one could say, in the semi-ecstatic recognition of the common—semi-ecstatic only because ecstasy's bliss may too easily preclude the strangely rigorous ethical nature of the experiment. It is an experiment—I like to remind myself as I like to remind my students—

that we cannot assume is over. The germ of that experiment reappraises the language that poetry might occur in; as Wordsworth describes it:

> The principal object, then, which I proposed to myself in these Poems was to chuse incidents and situations from common life, and to relate or describe them, throughout, as far as was possible, in a selection of language really used by men. . . . Low and rustic life was generally chosen, because in that condition, the essential passions of the heart find a better soil in which they can attain their maturity, are less under restraint, and speak a plainer and more emphatic language; because in that condition of life our elementary feelings co-exist in a state of greater simplicity, and consequently may be more accurately contemplated, and more forcibly communicated . . . because in that condition the passions of men are incorporated with the beautiful and permanent forms of nature. The language, too, of these men is adopted . . . because such men hourly communicate with the best objects from which the best part of language is originally derived.[10]

The latticework overarching the crisis of Romantic epistemology—of experience impossibly preceding experience, and of the poem as the expression of that paradox—is a theory of language. That theory (predating the Russian Formalism it is so reminiscent of) seeks a use that can strip the language, and so the eyes whose habit language forms, of expectation, of easy recognition in which the mind overleaps existence by assuming the reality of what is "real."

It is the common that is strange. A common language bears within it the necessary conditions of its own use. A rustic life chosen as the object of poetic imitation allows access to a language whose meaning isn't simply referential in nature but relational in nature—a work language whose expressive source erupts from the ground whose command it gives to turn, to plow, to sow, to reap. It is an urgent language whose danger is deeply intertwined with its own mimetic root. The urgency is that the world is real, is material, and though it seems wholly false, merely "romantic," to claim for a word a reality as substantive as that of an ear of wheat, or the germ whose ponderous weight bends the ear back to the ground from which it sprang, it is Romantic to see that language inscribes in the human mind the process by which the wheat grows, is harvested, is ground, is baked into bread. It is just as Romantic to see that language is that yeast-like substance that allows the bread to rise, except this bread is a metaphorical bread, nonetheless sustaining, in which the unspeakable world rises through words into the world utterable, marking the division of *I think* from *I am*, claiming the division as a connection, forging the livid bond in which opposites coexist. It does so—as Emerson knows when he writes that "Every word was once a poem"—not because language functions via sense and reference but because every word contains in itself the poetic moment of first consciousness, the very moment of the child's song, when a word is not a definition, not a recognition, but a relation in which the reality of the world must be countered by the reality of the self in that world. This real world is dubious. To sing extends reality through that doubt the song simultaneously creates; to sing claims inside the real a life that makes of the real a value. Poetry is a human art because it is a living art. I don't mean that it is living because it is still being written; it is a living art because it contains words that are themselves a form of the life they name.

This living quality of language removes Keats from his identical self. It must be so. For Keats realizes—as if instinctually, as if innately—that Romanticism's most radical experiment isn't simply a return to a common language but the understanding that language is what is in common. A poem recognizes in ways the writer of the poem may find uncomfortable that the other is always as real, if not more real, than the self who speaks. The poem calls into doubt the writer of the poem by offering itself to an unknown other who must exist to receive the poem, to warrant the world it bears as a real world and, by doing so, claiming herself as real.

Language extends this relational bridge across which the poet cannot help but walk, but she does not walk as herself—she walks across as the other she seeks, for the bridge is a common bridge, and to walk upon it is to put mere identity aside and become more real by becoming anonymous. The self, Romanticism says, is a hybrid creature. It is the choral revelation, when to say *I* is to speak for All, and the report, as in the old tragedies, is to say what the world is and what it is in the world that has been done. It is to hear the report, to hear the news. Not the news as Ezra Pound might have it. Not the "news that stay[s] news." But the voices speaking in the wires, the humming wires, whose import isn't merely the words they carry but the wind that blows across those tense lines in the air, that epic wind, whose singing fills the gaps, whose song sings of the world's ceaseless morning ceaselessly, the song that thrills tranquil absence into a humming presence, whose voice can only be heard against the curious fact of our own.

Epistemic Flow

I like to think about those rivers coursing underground, swift currents hidden under the surface of the earth, like veins beneath the skin, I suppose, when the river surges up, it is not a wound but a spring—a spring like the one beside which young Pindar fell asleep, tired from the hunt, and woke to find some bees had built a hive inside his mouth. But who knows if such rivers exist? I don't. I've only encountered them in books, in poems, in ideas: a geography on loan. There's the Alph, Coleridge's opiate stream,

the sacred river, ran
Through caverns measureless to man
Down to a sunless sea[1]

whose name alone evokes the Hebrew letter *aleph*, initiatory vowel of the entire alphabet but that carries no sound of its own. Or so some say. Other scholars claim *aleph* is the sound of the throat opening to speak, making a fountain of that other hidden river, speech. There's also the river Styx, on whose agitated waters the gods themselves swear their oaths. And Acheron, across whose waters Charon rows—if they've remembered to carry with them a coin—the newly dead souls. That river of lamentation, Cocytus. And among the others, perhaps my favorite, the river Lethe, that river that undoes the mind, turns memory into oblivion, and quenches the thirst for truth, or the difficulty of knowledge, with forgetfulness, once you bend down at the bank and take a sip of its waters.

There is another river, too, not exactly underground, a river that is every river and so is also no river at all. Heraclitus describes it: "You cannot step in the same river twice." Sometimes I call that river Memory; sometimes I call that river Mind. When thought teases us out into helpless waters and threatens the life it promised to explain, when beloved faces have no features but a blur and one must add the detail back in, we find we have stepped into that river, that river inside us. And then there is the river I call Light, which fills the nightly emptied channels, those arroyos some call self, and through the eyes pours in another day.

· · ·

The etymology of *influence* comes from the Latin and means "a flowing in." That flowing in is both an astrological term speaking of that spiritual flow of ethereal forms into human life and the flow of water. As a principle, *influence* speaks to a radical relation between us and all we exist among, material realities but also the forces that inform those realities. But "realities" feels like a word that is not exactly right. I mean those gathered moments of intensity that seem, along with us, to endure for a time Time itself (that river Time), before the flow that forms them joins them wholly to its larger motion, and what is flows away into what was. Bodies, ideas, books; memories, love, children; the gifts of days, the gifts of night; the sun and the Milky Way, all have coursing within them the river Lethe, a river coursing also through *Aletheia*, Greek word for Truth, whose subterranean influence reminds the mind that oblivion flows inside all that once became obvious.

As a poet born in the later twentieth century, and writing across the millennium into this new one, I worry that our sense of influence has diminished and the flow of those mighty rivers has grown weaker. Ezra Pound's dictum "Make it new," in echo still urges certain assumptions of what marks poetic validity: eases of experiment, cleverness as innovation. But Heraclitus might view that Modernist advice in his ancient light and remind us that what is new isn't what is without precedent, isn't what hasn't been encountered before. He would point at a river— any river would do—and remind us that what always has been and still is, is what is new. There is no work that must be done to "make it new" other than to step in, to open eyes, to open mouth, by which I also mean to open mind—to find some way to let what flows flow in.

Socrates, in the *Cratylus*—the dialog in which he considers the origins of language—seeks out what rivers flow beneath the surface of words. For a time, his interest lingers in the various words for knowledge itself:

HERMOGENES: What is the word?

SOCRATES: Wisdom (φρόνησις); for it is perception (νόησις) and
flowing (ῥόος); or it might be understood as benefit (ὄνησις) of
motion (φοράς); in either case it has to do with motion.... And
ἐπιστήμη (knowledge) indicates that the soul which is of any
account accompanies (ἐπέται) things in their motion, neither
falling behind them nor running in front of them; therefore we
ought to enter an epsilon and call it ἐπιστήμη.... Certainly σοφία
(wisdom) denotes the touching of motion. This word is very
obscure and of foreign origin; but we must remember that the
poets often say of something which begins to advance rapidly
ἐσύθη (it rushed). There was a famous Laconian whose name was
Σοῦσ (Rush), for this is the Laconian word for rapid motion. Now
σοφία signifies the touching (ἔπαθη) of this rapid motion, the
assumption being that things are in motion.[2]

A subtle strain of irony: Socrates is explaining the occult etymologies of
the words for wisdom and knowing to Hermogenes, whose name means
"born of Hermes," the trickster god who gave to humans the alphabet
and so the language that from those letters followed. But beneath the
irony, and under the playful teasing out from words the hidden springs of
their meanings, a poetic realization meanders to the surface. It is, Socrates
claims, an understanding to which poets might come first, and though it
sounds simple, it is not: that all is in motion.

Wisdom touches that motion, and knowledge—at least, that knowledge I might hazard to call poetic—joins things in their motion, not falling behind, not getting ahead. The first implication involves the work of
reading. Rather than the effort to pull from a text some knowledge that
then becomes one's own—a possession of a sort, one to add to the accu-
mulated treasure as a miser adds another coin to the glimmering pile, a
selfish economy that reflects back to oneself the illusion of expertise—the
reader who reads wisely enters into a poem to catch up to the speed of its
current, joins the flow of the thought coursing just below the words, and
rather than place themself as net or sieve within the rush, hoping to catch
what lives in the flow, becomes the flow, and so is themself the life carried along in the larger motion. To emerge is, so strangely, so wondrously,

not to think alone—but the river that flowed through the poem has also dug its channel into you, and in that bewildering canyonland that might serve as an image of the entire self, another fold for thought and perception to flow through has been etched. The self, seen as in a map or from a height, is but that landscape such influences have carved—and when the storm comes, be it thunderclap of inspiration or flash flood of sudden vision, that moment's force fills the self that influence formed.

· · ·

So it is that the poets I care most for, and the poet I would most want to be, possess an unexpected anxiety when it comes to influence—not the anxiety that leads to drawing away from those voices that might overwhelm and subsume one's own but the anxiety to enter into those voices as fully as one can and to sing within another poet's song.

I'm not speaking of imitation, though perhaps there is no finer story to illustrate my point than Jorge Luis Borges's "Pierre Menard, Author of the *Quixote*." In the tale, the speaker, in the guise of literary scholar of (and friend to) Pierre Menard, offers a complete list of all the author wrote—a number of monographs on philosophers and poets, including those on Gottfried Wilhelm Leibniz and Paul Valéry, a translation of Francisco de Quevedo, and a number of poems, symbolist in nature, sonnet in form. The speaker goes on:

> This is the full extent (save for a few vague sonnets of occasion destined for Mme. Henri Bachelier's hospitable, or greedy, *album des souvenirs*) of the *visible* lifework of Pierre Menard, in proper chronological order. I shall turn now to the other, the subterranean, the interminably heroic production—the *oeuvre nonpareil*, the *oeuvre* that must remain—for such are our human limitations!—unfinished. This work, perhaps the most significant writing of our time, consists of the ninth and thirty-eighth chapters of Part I of *Don Quixote* and a fragment of Chapter XXII. I know that such a claim is on the face of it absurd; justifying that "absurdity" shall be the primary object of this note.[3]

Let me join in with this anonymous scholar in seeking to justify the absurdity of his claim by further clarifying the hopes of Pierre Menard himself:

Those who have insinuated that Menard devoted his life to writing a contemporary *Quixote* besmirch his illustrious memory. Pierre Menard did
not want to compose *another* Quixote, which surely is easy enough—he
wanted to compose *the* Quixote. Nor, surely, need one be obliged to note
that his goal was never a mechanical transcription of the original; he
had no intention of *copying* it. His admirable ambition was to produce a
number of pages which coincided—word for word and line for line—with
those of Miguel de Cervantes. (39).

This ambition, which at first blush seems laughable, later seems a sober
miracle. Genius is pulled from the intimate confines of a single personality and is revealed instead as a common source, available to all—or to any
of those who are willing to do the subterranean work of digging down
beneath the surface to seek the source. There it is one finds the coursing
river not yet named, the river Influence. To enter it is to lose oneself, to
lose one's voice, or to learn to listen differently, so that one's own words
are but the echo of what other mouths are saying, as in the Greek chorus
of old, where *I* is a word that says *All*.

None of these ideas are new, nor are they meant to be. I am not a poet,
nor a thinker, who wants to "Make it new." To tell the truth, I don't know
what that imperative means. Plutarch claimed of Socrates that he could
hear the voices articulate in the air, a vision by which I've come to suspect
that every utterance from a human life still speaks itself above us, and
the gathering clouds on any given day are a conversation, and the atmosphere is just an opportunity to eavesdrop. But there is a counter side to
the same fact, an influential articulation deep in the chthonic rivers that
shape within each of us whatever it is that intelligence and perception
come to be in a given life. If it is so, and if one can dig down within oneself (Paul Celan: "There was earth in them, and they dug.") deep enough,
one can find that necessity of thinking that urged the great works of literature to become what they became, and only an arrogant fool would
think that once the book or poem is written the source within it is gone.
How could it be so? Then, like a tree whose root taps down into empty
aquifer in a land of drought, the life would wither and offer no fruit. But
this tree of knowledge, rooted in influence, so awfully and full of awe
blooms.

• • •

I know there were rivers running through Eden, and though I've forgotten their names, I have my suspicions that those waters still flow. If so, they carry something still of Adam's mythic act of naming—no arbitrary effort, not cleverness or willful act, but simply a seeing the deep signature in all things and saying for them the name they cannot speak themselves. Perhaps it is what is too easily forgotten, and whose consequences become selfishly lamentable, that no one needs to make their own language—it is already there, speaking.

How to speak with it is the influential question. For John Keats, it required the realization that the poet's self was no self at all:

> As to the poetical Character itself (I mean that sort of which, if I am anything, I am a Member; that sort distinguished from the wordsworthian or egotistical sublime, which is a thing per se and stands alone), it is not itself—it has no self—it is everything and nothing—It has no character.... What shocks the virtuous philosopher, delights the camelion poet. It does no harm from its relish of the dark side of things any more than from its taste for the bright one; because they both end in speculation. A Poet is the most unpoetical of any thing in existence; because he has no Identity—he is continually in for—and filling some other Body—The Sun, the Moon, the Sea and Men and Women who are creatures of impulse are poetical and have about them an unchangeable attribute—the poet has none; no identity—he is certainly the most unpoetical of all God's Creatures. If then he has no self, and if I am a Poet, where is the Wonder that I should say I would write no more? Might I not at that very instant have been cogitating on the Characters of Saturn and Ops? It is a wretched thing to confess; but [it] is a very fact that not one word I ever utter can be taken for granted as an opinion growing out of my identical nature—how can it, when I have no nature? When I am in a room with People if I ever am free from speculating on creations of my own brain, then not myself goes home to myself: but the identity of every one in the room begins so to press upon me that I am in a very little time annihilated—not only among Men; it would be the same in a Nursery of children.[4]

The end of such annihilation isn't death but a poem. It is one composed not of one's identical self—though the vestiges of the helpless fact of living one's own life cannot help but inform the work that springs up within it—but of those realities that have so pressed up within the writer that make his mouth their own. Such is the effort that influence might require of us whose dearest wish is to write what already has been written (and, I admit, I'm one of that number): to let the unchangeable attributes of what is not us give to us their shape. The poet's open mouth, that invocatory O, is also the mouth of the cave deep within which Influence flows. One way to write is to walk straight into the poet's mouth.

And so I try—

• • •

ODE TO A—

1.

I wake. Sometimes it's that simple. Numb
   In the morning's dumb cloud-muted light
I hear the rain fall drop by drop into the plum
   Tree growing purple rocks, bruises that delight
The eye, high on the highest branch, but leave
   The mind empty as the empty mouth. O—
For a mouthful of that—. Almost all of it is out of reach.
   Little alarm bell of the thrush's throat, leave
Your song alone. Learn as I've learned. Let it go.
   Beauty thinks in fevers. Sings an ache it likes to teach.

2.

From deep within the tree the lesson starts.
   At the students' approach, the teacher
Departs. It's how I learned to tighten my heart
   Into a book with a clasp no key opens, fair
Warning to anyone who fears each page
   Must be blank. It works if it beats. It works
If between its covers it keeps its heat.
   To ask it your question requires the lost age
Return new. That can't happen. I've tried to jerk
   The centuries back with a word or two, to cheat

3.
Time with sweet rhymes, to make a bird a chime
    That in the gloom behind the eye rings true.
Here I've sat somehow inside myself, time
    Beginning to turn a few hairs gray, youth
No longer young. There's a simple thing I want
    To say, but the words don't work right,
Don't ease this maze of mind back into a bower,
    But sorrow thought more intricate, taint
The bright eye with lead. Even the sunlight
    Mocks what it brightens, murmuring tomorrow,
4.
Darkens the moment's shine as shade gathers
    Deep within the leaves—where thrush, you sing—
Long before dusk rushes the shadows in, long before
    A feather from a hectic breast goes missing
In the uncut, full-of-night, grass. Love too is lost.
    Love walks in the dark on a palsied foot
Reciting lines memorized long ago about the toil
    Of old heroes who died, ocean-tossed,
After crushing ancient towers into dust, not
    Not knowing what else to do, but die—.
5.
I cannot see what flowers are at my feet.
    I wouldn't know their names if I could.
Memory litters the dark with words grown sweet
    In the mouth. To say one out loud
Forms in the dark a little cloud that rains
    Down sense. White eglantine. Musk rose.
They hum in the ear like the flies that haunt
    The honey they sip. It takes so much pain
To see what is not there to see. To breathe deep in
    The missing scent. So you sing, I suppose.
6.
And I listen. I try to sing along. To quiet
    Death into a child's game a child fears

But not for long, where death dies and quits
    The charade, stands up, wipes away tears
And says, it's okay. You choose your gloom.
    Emperors have heard this same song;
So has my mother, Ruth, teaching her students
    Division in public school classrooms,
Speaking softly to the dim child, the answer's wrong,
    Try again. Getting it right comes by accident.
7.
I'm trying again. The same thing I always try.
    To hear the thrush sing abroad its soul
In such an ecstasy—. Not an irony.
    Melody that deep in the blood tolls
Now as always it's tolled, heart-bell
    That breaks the mind with ringing, ringing—
Thrush, I hear you, you sing it out as always
    It's been sung, to fathers as to sons, to tell
All what we would rather not know. Singing
    Removes you from the song, it finds a way
8.
To be sung again, by another mouth, by other
    Wings than yours. Forlorn. The word
Weighs down my tongue as years before
    It brooded down another's. Fate has one cure:
To repeat the music even as it flees, or is fled
    Already, always, perfect seed of the ever-past
Tense. For just a moment, just a song sung deep
    Within these fading leaves, I think I lived.
I think so. I'm not sure. It didn't last—
    my fraction of day sung in dreamless sleep.

Lyric Consciousness

My youngest daughter's name is Iris. Kristy and I chose it for all its meanings: she was born at the end of May, when the irises in our yard bloom, the colored ring of the eye, and that ancient goddess, first messenger of the Olympians, who also bore the responsibility of watering the clouds, and so, so it is said, her wings were made of rainbows. But I never knew her lineage until recently, returning to Plato's dialog on the nature of knowledge, the *Theaetetus*. It comes after Theaetetus admits that the conversation confuses him. The young man says, "I am lost in wonder when I think of all these things, and sometimes when I regard them it really makes my head swim." Socrates responds, "This feeling of wonder shows that you are a philosopher, since wonder is the only beginning of philosophy, and he who has said that Iris is the child of Thaumos made a good genealogy."[1] Thaumos is the god of Wonder. And so it seems that the very child who speeds the gods' messages from lip to ear, from heaven to earth, accomplishes something Wonder cannot achieve himself—she can put into words what stuns the mind to silence, can give image to what so strikes the mind that the mind stands agape and astonished, lets us imagine that beauty that obliterates consideration, and so consider it, in the words of the message.

These days I have been wondering about images. My oldest daughter, Hana, takes photos of herself on her phone and finds herself there looking back. My students update the image of their status in the middle of class. Going to buy apples at the grocery store I find me hovering above myself on the surveillance screen. The magazines at checkout consider the consequences of lives lived out in reality-based television shows. Real housewives of—. Dancing with stars—. Conspiracy theories of the new tsar—. A president who likes to watch himself watch himself on TV, as in the dizzying, eternal repetitions, each image smaller than the last as it extends out to infinity, of standing between two mirrors facing each other—.

Another image—. I imagine it like this: at day, the voice speaks out from a column of smoke; at night, the voice speaks out from a column of flame. These are the years of desert wandering, of manna eating, of having escaped by walking through a divided sea. In Exodus God says, "Thou shalt not make unto thee any graven image, or any likeness of any thing that is in heaven above, or that is in the earth beneath, or that is in the water under the earth."[2] That command for many years felt to me base and cruel, evidence of some God I wanted no part of, jealous and vindictive. What is there to fear, I thought, when you are yourself absolute fear, and absolute love, power, and knowledge, and complete presence? But now I hear that voice speak out from the dark smoke about something deep in human nature; now I hear the voice speak out from flame not a threat but warning us against ourselves. The image that turns idol. Baal's golden ram. Oscar's golden man. The fate inside the image, I mean, its fatality: stilling infinite forces into a token, making of power a coin for exchange, replacing the lost face of the loved one with an amulet on a chain, and of any life lost—the animal hunted or the animal sacrificed, the child put on an altar at demand of the goddess, the poet panting above the poem—how it is we worship the thing our own hands made, and put the object of our faith in the place of faith, and desire most to possess that by which we should ourselves be possessed. We love to feel ourselves love. But is that love? Or is it just a category, listed somewhere in the endless annals of the museum library, simply titled "The Forms of Love," a treatise in many volumes, illustrated throughout, that we can borrow for a while, a few months or years, or for a life entire? A book one doesn't even read. Just cherishes. Just holds. Just carries around. I wonder.

Other stories from other traditions clasp on to the warning in Exodus, a kind of charm bracelet in the head. Socrates, who at first admired the winged madness of poets, later bans them from his republic, for the poems paint false images of the gods and, worse, teach us to love falsehoods more than we love truth; then, centuries later, a young man named Cleombrotus says good-bye to the sun and jumps from a wall down into Hades, for he had read just once Plato's treatise *On the Soul*. King Midas wanders through the mind, and any thought he touches turns to gold. There is the Gorgon there too—to be caught by her gaze is to turn into stone. Except now we are the ones who want to be seen; we are the ones trying to catch Medusa's eye. Except now each of us is King Midas, but we only touch ourselves. Outside my window the storm clouds come in over the mountains, dark as smoke. Is that laughter or is that thunder in the cloud?

· · ·

The horror of the Gorgon's gaze may not be the death she causes but, rather, the astonished accuracy of the life stilled into stone, so lifelike you might convince yourself that any breeze is a breath from marble lips, so lifelike you might see a pulse in the press of the vein beneath the alabaster skin. So, too, of Midas: the gold seems alive. But of Baal's ram and other idols, the error isn't their uncanny accuracy (according to ancient sources now lost so that only the rumor exists, Baal's golden ram was no more than a lump of clay whose silica content made it shine golden in the sun and whose shape was made by the imprint of the hand that clenched it) but some other sense of definition. It is, after all, the "graven" image that is forbidden. The word's root digs literally down: to *dig*, to *bury*. Hearing it so reveals the threat. Not God's forbidding warning. But that the *graven image* is one of death's most subtle forms: the death that mimics life, the death that acts like life. It says: the consequence of form is mortality.

It is a fool's path, I know, but I like to think my relationship to anything could be infinite. It is a foolish thought, but an age-old one, that poetry traffics in eternity. The question becomes a simple-seeming one, but I fear it's simple in the way the center of a maze is simple—a clearing, yes; a clarity, yes; but there are still the obscure paths. What's strangest is that you might well have to build the obscurity yourself, build the maze and build the darkness. You might have to teach yourself how to get lost.

One way to begin, is to begin in error:

By my Window have I for scenery
Just a Sea—with a Stem—
If the Bird and the Farmer—deem it a "Pine"—
The opinion will serve—for them—

It has no Port, nor a "Line"—but the Jays—
That split their route to the Sky—

Or a Squirrel, whose giddy Peninsula
May be easier reached—this way—

For Inlands—the Earth is the under side—
And the upper side—is the Sun—
And its Commerce—if Commerce it have—
Of Spice—I infer from the Odors borne—[3]

Miracle here is mistake's dearest form. A world forms within the world and upends the inherited order. Now the sea perches on a stem, and the ocean that to Dickinson's Bird or Farmer must stretch out horizontal to the horizon is outside the poet's window a vertical presence linking its inland earth to the sun. A breeze brings the scent of the spicy isles, and should the wind become a gale, the waves will shake loose their spray of pollen. Dickinson lets her senses bewilder her rationality, accepts the accident of eye and nose for an insight into the world that also radically redefines it. The effort isn't to deem the pine recognizable. The hope is to betray the ease of our definition, and so short-circuit that idolatrous turn within the human urge to represent, to categorize, to replace presence with an image, to pack infinity into a frame. Listen to Dickinson listen:

Of its Voice—to affirm—when the Wind is within—
Can the Dumb—define the Divine?
The Definition of Melody—is—
That Definition is none—[4]

Her every sense works not to dispel error but to dwell more deeply within it. That "Wind within" is more than inspiration; it is that *pneuma*, that *spiritus*, that coursing through the entirety of creation ignores the boundaries that make any given object singular, undoing that illusion of solitude to make a wilder claim. What is the claim? I don't exactly know. It's a world that leaves me wordless; a melody or a music hard to hear because it isn't played to me—I'm just one of the instruments the wind blows through. That's why I have a reed for a tongue. That's why my mind is just a set of holes that change the pitch of the tune.

So it may be, Dickinson suggests, that the best way to see clearly is to close one's eyes:

It—suggests to our Faith—
They—suggest to our Sight—
When the latter—is put away
I shall meet with Conviction I somewhere met
That Immortality—[5]

Putting sight away creates an image of a different kind, one not graven into that form of vision that confuses seeing with knowing and knowing with possessing. Don't deem this "Sea—with a stem" a "Pine" tree. To do so is faithless certainty. There is another economy the cost of which is not bond nor debt, unless breathing is a debt; unless inspiration is currency; and then the resin scent reveals what should have always been obvious, save the fact had been hidden in the maze of our habitual definitions, and we could not see it because we kept seeing it—the pine as a pine—that in our own yard the sea stands up straight, making a new economy between sun and soil, heaven and earth. Then the real question can be asked:

Was the Pine at my Window a "Fellow
Of the Royal" Infinity?
Apprehensions—are God's introductions—
To be hallowed—accordingly—[6]

• • •

For many years those last two lines have repeated themselves in my mind. Even when I forgot to say them to myself, they spoke themselves in me. Maybe that's thinking, what says itself in you, what uses you to say itself and cannot be said in any other way: "Apprehensions—are God's introductions— / To be hallowed—accordingly—." *Apprehension* is a curious word, and Dickinson means it in all its simultaneous curiosity: to *fear*, to *grasp*, to *understand*. It gives to knowing a trembling complexity that does not seem like knowing. It makes thinking feel like something other than thinking—the hand reaching out, desiring and afraid of what it might find, wanting to grasp or to be grasped—in other words, the gesture of introduction. Among the various verbs for "knowing" in Greek, the most instructive I've found is apprehensive in its nature. The word is λαμβάνω, and it means *to take hold of, grasp, seize (bodily and emotionally); to overtake; to apprehend by the senses; to apprehend with the mind, to understand; to take in hand, to receive.* More than reciprocity informs the word. As true as it is to suggest it implies that the hand reaching out to take is also reaching out to receive, it also suggests that the senses work as the mind's ever-opening hands, it also hints that passion is an epistemology and that the mind isn't that ratio behind the eyes comparing the names to one another, but the mind drifts down to open palm, and the mind drifts through the heart, and the mind is a vessel adrift in the current of the pine tree's scent. Then thinking makes of the mind that form of apprehensiveness called *threshold*, that gap in definition, that hole in boundary, that door in dwelling, that marks the very place of introduction—not simply a greeting but the realization that each of us is always at the beginning of our relation to each other and to the world. Always initial, initiating. Always being introduced.

What it is to write within the space of such hallowed introduction, to work in words so as to become apprehensive, means thinking itself must be thought about—a riddling proposition the maze of which is propositional, occurring sentence by sentence, word by word. Heidegger, in his beautiful and bewildering essay "What Calls for Thinking?" begins with a simple enough point: "We learn to think by giving heed to what there is to think about."[7] Thinking here aligns itself with existence in lovely echo of Parmenides—that the path we can speak of is the one that is there. Heidegger posits that fundamental reality is at the core of thinking differently than as a road and the teleology inherent in the image—that there is a place to arrive at, a determined point, a fated knowing, destiny or destination. Instead, he describes what we seek to hold in the mind as a protective instinct, as "letting a herd graze at pasture."[8] The grass, I guess, is food enough for thought. But Heidegger knows, too, that as with the herd at pasture, the creatures turn away to other meadows when one steps near or, as he puts it, "what must be thought about turns away."[9] The question about thinking is not how to find an answer but how to "be admitted into questions that seek what no inventiveness can find."[10] We are drawn along by what draws away, pointing after the departure, and that gesture is no cleverness of intellect but, rather, the necessary image of thought itself. It points, but pointing is not enough. The eyes reach farther along the line the finger points out, and the mind thinks further than sight, but neither finger nor eye nor mind can beckon back that herd grazing now at the distant meadow called horizon. For that hope—so

simple as to dismantle the pride a person might feel in being "smart"—
that one can learn to think about what is there to be thought about, what
calls out for our thinking, that meadow that, as the poet Robert Duncan
has it, is a "scene made-up by the mind, / that is not mine, but is a made
place, // that is mine, it is so near to the heart, / an eternal pasture folded
in all thought."[11] *Fold* is a thoughtful word—a gentle curve in the ground;
a pen or enclosure for animals; a crease in a page—and a word it seems is
what's needed. A word that, like the arrow shot from the bow's string, is
cast out by the taut lyre string of mind not to wound the animal aimed
at by thinking toward it but to call back to what calls out to us and so
make a fold, a patch of grass right near the heart, where whatever thinking is, whatever that herd is, can graze and in grazing be. Then we are in
the proper alignment to the words we use. Not inventors, not creators.
Then it is as Heidegger says, "It is not we who play with words; rather, the
essence of language plays with us."[12]

To be in the hands of language, to be the object of its apprehension,
obliterates consideration as we used to know it—we say to ourselves, *I do
not know how to think; I just think I've been thinking*. To be in the apprehension of language is to realize that thinking isn't something *I do* but something that happens *to me*. It is to be struck—not as the creature that by the
arrow is struck but as the string of the lyre is. Struck so that a note plays—a
vibration in air and mind, in memory and myth, in moment and slow
time, whose grace is to draw into sympathy radically different realms of
experience. Heidegger casts this hope to "radically unlearn what thinking
has been" in ancient terms—that we must learn to keep intact the relation
of μῦθος to λόγος. Heidegger defines *μῦθος* in a simple and lovely way:
"what has its essence in its telling." The word λόγος is of such complexity
it bears offering a portion of its meanings: *accounting, reckoning; measure,
tale; esteem, consideration, value; relation, correspondence, proportion, ratio;
statement of theory, argument, proposition, rule; thesis, hypothesis, provi-
sional ground* ... and the list goes much further, bringing into relief a subtle but overwhelming sense that λόγος is a word hovering above or beside
reality, thinking *of* or *apart from* rather than thinking *within*, theorizing
life and world rather than apprehending them. The word λόγος needs no
"introductions" in Dickinson's sense, for it assumes that whatever God is,
God has left, and what was hallowed is now hollowed, and that god-like/
un-god-like thing can take its place, that thing we call thinking.

But to keep μῦθος and λόγος twinned and twined ravels again the untwisted tendrils sprung out from the root of the mind. Words drop from their ratios into their essential telling—a fecund and fearsome speaking, where Memory herself sows the field, where the grazing herd wanders into being even as it wanders away, and nothing knows how to keep itself pure and apart—not the animal from Aesop's tale, not the goddess and her namesake child, not the raindrop from the prism, not light from bow. Here the world reclaims its symbolic nature in the midst of its daily reality, here in this meadow—where sometimes I am permitted to return. The cost of that permission? A kind of leap, as Heidegger says, that takes us to what "will confound us"—a leap, I might say, into that fold that is the apprehensive page. The words that fill that page, the furrows of those lines and sentences, proceed along laws different from those that λόγος alone establishes. Argument withers. Theory's husk winnows away. Reason grows wary of its own ratios. In place of those various logics a mind takes root. It is in part the mind of the one who writes the essay or poem; but it is also the mind held by the bounds of the meadow, the bounds of the fold, a thinking thing that thinks itself and, in so doing, unfurls a leaf that so catches the eye with its bright green that we think along with it, an aspect of the thought itself. All those thoughts that gather what light they can. All those eyes that are leaves. Lyric consciousness plays its tune along the grass harp when the wind blows and makes of song, sense. Those are the pages I want to read, those that invite everything in to think, and in listening in, in feeling that we ourselves don't know how to think, not exactly, begin to learn to do so. This page, this field, is the very region of what is most thought-provoking, where, as Heidegger says, we learn "that we still are not thinking; none of us, including me who speaks to you, me first of all."[13]

• • •

Listen to me. I'm finishing this essay I've spent many weeks on while sitting in the gazebo in my backyard. Behind me, just today, the first iris has bloomed. It is a flower comprised of six purple tongues that grow yellow at the throat, and hidden inside them are three more tongues the color of pale dawn. I had my fingers in its mouth, so I know. Though mid-May heavy snow is predicted tomorrow. Who will tell the iris if not Iris herself? Daughter or goddess, either will do. Her father lives deep inside some blankness, sleeps between white sheets, wakes to cloud and sky, spends his days wondering; her father, Wonder. I know there's something to say. Some words to speak. But I also know they must speak themselves. Imagine themselves.

Then Midas can touch what he touches without it turning to gold.

Then the Gorgon can watch the children play.

Then the image isn't graven—and the fire goes calm, and the smoke stays quiet.

For then the essay is no idol of knowledge, thinking it knows how to think. It just thinks. I think it thinks. But I'm dizzy and lost in wonder when I think of all these things, and sometimes when I regard them it really makes my head swim. Just like Theaetetus working so hard to think about thinking that he hardly knows what he knows. He and Socrates try so hard. They come up with a beautiful image—an image of apprehension. They imagine the mind as an aviary, and each bird there is a kind of knowledge. Which one you grab, you learn, you know. Hold enough birds in your hands, and you end up knowledgeable. I suppose those birds in flight are what I might call thinking. I like to think if you hold out your hand long enough, a bird might simply perch there, or make of your palm a kind of nest. I can imagine it that way, thinking coming to the open hand.

I like that image. It makes me happy.

But there is one more aspect to apprehension I'd like to add, one more aspect to thinking and how it relates to knowledge. Theaetetus makes a wonderful suggestion to Socrates. "Perhaps, Socrates," he says, "we were not right in making birds represent kinds of knowledge only, but we ought to have imagined kinds of ignorance also flying about in the soul with the others; then the hunter would catch sometimes knowledge and sometimes ignorance of the same thing."[14] In one hand knowledge; in the other oblivion. So it is I've learned the writer is one who walks with both hands stretched out before themself, learning how to know and also not know what they know—how to forget to think, how to discover in the hand not an image of truth or beauty, but a bird, a bird, whose name I can almost remember, a name I know, that name I can't recall.

The Road Up Is the Road Down

(Kenyon College/Naropa University June 2023)

A poem is a double work, I feel it as I never have before: that a poem gives us new eyes. A poem gives us two new eyes that seem the same but see differently: one sees the day, and one sees under the day—and every poem, or every poem of a certain nature, walks the surface of the world and walks under it at the same time. It's hard to know who it is you are: the poet singing a solar ode or the poet reminding the shades there is a sun. Both poets are one but not the same. The difference is as hard to point at as it is to name, self and self's shadow, maybe, but only if we understand that the body is a projection of the shadow as truly as the shadow is a silhouette of the body. Properly seen, neither is more substantial than the other: the hand, the shadow of the hand; the hand, the other-hand. So of day and other-day; so of night and other-night. Honestly, it all makes me want to weep, but I'm trying not to. There are students, and others, wanting to think that poetry is something other than what brings you to tears. But, you know, I'm not sure it is. To offer sorrow as joy, as also joy; or if not joy, as wonder. To wonder with a wonder pulled up from the dark inside the dark is a work that—even if it ends in failure, even if it must fail, even if love herself must say "farewell" and walk backward down the road she just walked up—is worthiest labor. To work in wonder toward wonder's wonder, in bewilderment toward bewilderment's wilds. And everyone is weeping anyway inside themselves, and it's only decency, isn't it, to point it out? To point out, or at, the nature of our work: these new eyes, their ancient tears.

The poet's ancient tool is the lyre. It makes of lyric poems even now a sung thing. To write a lyric poem is a strange rehearsal, a choir practice, an audition asking if you, too, might be worthy enough to join the chorus, that ancient group wandering through tragedies they cannot stop but can sing of, can sing with; who say I, but I is multiple, I is us all. Selves inside the self, suggesting quietly to our ears even now—for those of us who would be lyric poets—that our most intimate self is also our most anonymous. Not so much an identity as a place; not so much a personality as a threshing ground. Sometimes we hear a whisper inside ourselves, echoing inside ourselves, in that cavern, in that underworld, asking us to sing what it says. The invention of the lyre is weird in the deepest etymology of the word: a form of destiny whose unexpected fate always arrives at the threshold of song, the mouth, the lips, where the inner logic leaps out and becomes living myth. For the Greeks, words were winged: they flew out from the mouth alive: Homer as columbarium. Hermes made the lyre on the day of his birth:

Indeed, he didn't lie around in his sacred cradle, no, the minute he slipped from his mother's immortal arms he leapt up and set out to find Apollo's herds. As he crossed the threshold of that roomy cave, he happened on a turtle and got himself an endless source of wealth. For you should know that it was Hermes who first made the turtle into something that could sing. Their paths crossed at the courtyard gate, where the turtle was waddling by, chewing the thick grass in front of the dwelling. Hermes, the bringer of luck, took a close look, laughed, and said:

"Here's a bit of luck I can't ignore! Hello there, you shapely thing, dancing girl, life of the party. Lovely to see you. How'd a mountain girl with a shiny shell get so playful? Let me carry you inside! What a blessing! Do me a favor, come on, I'll respect you. It's safer inside, you could get in trouble out there. A living turtle, they say, keeps troubling witchcraft away. And yet, if you were to die you'd sing most beautifully."

So saying, Hermes picked up the turtle with both hands and carried his lovely toy into the house. He turned her over and with a scoop of gray iron scraped the marrow from her shell. And, just as a swift thought can fly through the heart of a person with a haunted care, just as bright glances spin from the eyes, so, in one instant, Hermes knew what to do and did it. He cut stalks of reed to measure, fitted them through the shell, and fastened their ends across the back. Skillfully, he tightened a piece of cowhide, set the arms in place, fixed a yoke across them, and stretched seven sheep-gut strings to sound in harmony.

When he was finished, he took that lovely thing and tested each string in turn with a flat pick. It rang out wonderfully at the touch of his hand, and he sang along beautifully, improvising a few random snatches the way teenagers sing out insults at a fair.[1]

"And yet, if you were to die you'd sing most beautifully." It's a contradiction so troubling, a paradox so profound, it threatens to break the mind that birthed it—until you realize, it's the paradox that birthed the mind, not the other way around. The condition to sing beautifully is first to die; only then can the song be beautiful. Harmony is haunted. An ancient word, "harmony," or ἁρμονία, refers not to simultaneously sounded musical notes creating a chord but to a "joint," a "jointure," as of dovetailing in carpentry, fitting two pieces of wood together, no nail or glue needed to keep the joint sound.

The lyre's harmony is of phenomenological depth. It's there in the bedrock obscurity of the mind, so it comes as no surprise that Heraclitus the Obscure focuses on it as an object of primary importance. He notes it three times. He writes, "They cannot see how what draws itself apart pulls itself together: bending back is the harmony of bow and lyre."[2] Imagine the bow's taut string drawn back, and being drawn back, the far ends of the bow nearly bend into a circle. So it is one of lyric's miraculous transformations that the bow string *I* turns into the poet's oracular *O*. The lyre and the bow operate by the same principle, and deep irony lurks here too. Heraclitus: "The bow has the name of life and is the work of death." We need different ears to hear the pun. In ancient Greek one of the words for bow is βιός, accent on the second syllable; the word for life is βίος, accent on the first. Here harmony's jointure is sonic, bow and life dovetailed into one strange and fated tool. The principle holds to vaster territory than lyric practice; or, lyric practice is a vaster territory than we imagined. Heraclitus: "As of the lyre and the bow, the cosmos is a harmony drawn back."[3]

It's a tool that suggests, as baby Hermes knows, that death and song are a one as weird as we ourselves are a one—manifold but singular, self-same but myriad. So, too, of origin and end. The ease of time's straight line drawn between birth and death is a different geometry when the poet's hand draws back the taut string; then it becomes a circle. Figure of eternal return, of Omega's helpless investment in Alpha, that makes of the poem not a song flung toward specific meaning, not a self-expression, but a vibration, a frequency, that makes of the air itself an invisible hut you find yourself within only for as long as you hear the song—voice's instant merged with death's infinitive, eternity pitches its tent inside the ear. You step in profane, and when the song ends, you find yourself cast out, as if born again, with new eyes open to the world as sacred whole. So we hear of Thales, first philosopher in the Greek tradition, this anecdote:

"Death," he said, "is no different than life." "If so," someone said, "why don't you die?" "Because there is no difference," he said.[4]

Philosophy's roots are entangled with poetry's—the earliest philosophers wrote in Homer's hexameters. Sappho lived at the same time as Thales and not far away, on the island of Lesbos off the coast of what now is Turkey, where Thales lived in the seaside town of Miletus. She begins a love poem in this lyric harmony: "I honestly wish I'd died."[5]

Hermes made the lyre, and to appease Apollo, whose holy cattle the infant stole, the trickster gives the sun-god his favorite toy. Apollo is prophet-poet, god of Delphi, whose words riddle the truth they also reveal. Hermes sings a different art, one of cunning, one that speaks truth as easily as it deceives, that blurs the line between fable and fact, and prophesizes only in the minor key, telling others what the bee maidens tell him. But if the lyre were an instrument tuned only to the hands of a god, it would have no human meaning, not really—just another wonder, like the sun, like the stars, like knowledge, like truth, that doesn't get to be ours but drifts through us, a kind of mood. Yet the lyre is also fitted to human hands, might fit better in human hands. And Orpheus, archetypal poet, plays the lyre. Orpheus grasping the lyre, learning to play it, fitting his hands to the form, fitting his hands to the strings or plectrum, doesn't so much rip the tool from the hands of the gods as he discovers it anew, as if never found before, and in finding the lyre, he finds something more surprising: he discovers his own hands. It's easy to think that the hands hold the object, but it's a profane thought. Dismantle the edifice of our pride, and we sense something closer to the truth: that the tool grasps our hands and, in doing so, gives them back to us. Strange harmony, the jointure of hand to handle, a two that is a one, that teaches us the hidden fact of our nature, that alone we are less than whole, and we need some other, any other, but an other heedfully approached, to complete us.

What Heidegger says of the hammer speaks also of the lyre: "The less we just stare at the thing called hammer, the more we take hold of it and

use it, the more original our relation to it becomes and the more undis-
guisedly it is encountered as what it is, as a useful thing."[6] The lyre is a
useful thing. I think I've spent most of my life trying to understand the
nature of its usefulness—which cannot be a theory but can only be found
by using it, over and over again, realizing that the truest result of having
written a poem is simply the need to make another and finding yourself,
somehow, more able to do so. But Heidegger also gives us the mystery
of the work. Mastery of a tool doesn't result in the fluent knowledge of
how to use it to make anything it is you want to make. No. That fluency
is what must be put aside. To master the tool is to be mastered by it. The
hand knows itself by holding the tool. Poetry gives us two eyes. One eye
sees that the hand builds the tool; the other-eye sees that the tool makes
the hand that makes the tool. How important it is—though how impossible—to see with both eyes at once I don't think I can stress enough.
Maybe because I don't know it fully enough myself to stress it. But what I
suspect, or what I seem to half see, is this: the more work we do, the closer
we get to being able to begin our work. Our relation grows more original.
More capable of origin. How can it be that after writing poems for thirty
years I'm still waiting to write my first one? I keep wondering if I'm ready
yet to write that first poem. Sometimes I put my hand against my throat
and hum simply to feel the vibration. It seems to remind me of something I haven't forgotten enough to truly remember. This vibration in the
hand. This frequency. I think it's called a poem. A poem of infinitely small
vocabulary. A hum—. A poem—.

• • •

A tool works on material, and the raw stuff of poetry is words themselves.
Breath only breathes without words; but with words, breath sings. Can
sing. And in the strange fatefulness poetry forever initiates us into, we
can suspect, we singers in the chorus, that the breath given to language is
a kind of offering, a sacrifice in the ancient sense, that lends to breathless
words the very substance they need to live again. It's a variation of the
same principle, lyric speech, as the wine poured into a pit, as the blood
poured into a pitkin, given to ghosts and spirits both to appease and to
avert. The words in ancient Greek for "word" are manifold and instructive.
I want to put *logos* aside, most famous of them all, whose definition runs
through the small type of the midnight blue Liddell and Scott dictionary

for many pages. Humbler words open other vastnesses. There is *epos*, a word from which we get "epic." Pause on the word rather than sprint past it, and patience reveals something that feels long known but seldom recognized: that every word is itself an epic. Of course it is. Every word we say bears within it the countless iterations of its being said before, has in-folded within its very syllables complexities of feeling and thought that outstrip the experience of any single life. Even that humblest of words, the indefinite article *a*, holds within it the ever-more-urgent need to point at something in the world and ask if it exists or suggests that it does. A dandelion. A weeping willow. A nuthatch. The word *a* is one of the worthiest poems I know, easy to memorize but an endless song.

The word *mnema* means not only "word" but "record, memorial, remembrance." The word *sema* angles similarly, meaning "sign, mark, token," but deeper down in the etymology, it also means "sign by which a grave is known, mound, cairn, barrow." Language isn't only earthly stuff but under-earthly. A paean sings a dirge; an epithalamium has, for those who can hear it, a lament sobbing inside it. This isn't morose; it's accurate. Language speaks to the living, is the primary tool of the living, a *techne* never eclipsed in terms of its human importance; and yet, language is also a burial ground, a funeral mound, a daily repetition of facts that archaeologists have long known: that as first houses were built on the graves of ancestors so that the loved and lost could still be in the home, still offer their wisdom, their love, their advice, so a poem is built on the graves of the ancestors for the very same reasons and the very same hopes. Indeed, the poem is a hut made of those graves.

If the lyre gives Orpheus his hands, we might also see with our other eye that the mind doesn't make words, but words make the mind. Only then are we brought into our proper relation to the material our art is made of, more passive than active, performing our work weirdly against ourselves, a grammatical voice we do not have in English but the ancient Greeks did, a voice called the *middle voice*, where some verbs change their meaning, and the noun from which poet comes, and the verb cognate with it—which means merely "to make, to do"—transforms in the middle voice into "to consider." You cannot think the poem's thoughts outside the poem, at least not before the poem is written. The poem must be made before the thinking can begin. Before the thinking can begin, we must see that our words for "word" themselves promise that the mind is other than we ever imagined it. Not only the fine sieve of the present tense but more, far more, a version, or a vision, of the underworld itself, where the shades wander among the shadow-orchards, waiting for a breath and someone, anyone, even you, to sing for them their songs. Such are the rites, initiate, into the lesser mysteries, these rites of the lyric poem.

. . .

Ritual restores to wholeness what has fallen apart. Orpheus married Eurydice, a ritual that mends partial selves into something larger than either alone, a more-than-self self, bewildering in its own right but beautiful. But the ceremony had bad omens—the bridal torches sputtered and smoked—and shortly after the vows were spoken, Eurydice stepped on a snake, the serpent bit her ankle, and she limped her way down the long road to hell. "Orpheus wept / within the upper world," Ovid says, "but when his share / of long lament was done,"[7] he took his lyre and learned to weep in a new way, not the weeping of the upper world but a weeping that grants you entrance to the lower, not—as we have our daylit grief—a sobbing that replaces words but a sobbing of night, deepest night, the other-night, where words themselves weep out their sorrow, so akin to our own, who know what it is to lose what you love most, words that so seldom get to be the things they ardently name. Words that weep with us.

A patient man might know death would also come to him, and what are years, even decades, to the eternity waiting for Orpheus, when once again Eurydice would be his wife? But "Orpheus is guilty of impatience,"[8] as Maurice Blanchot says. Eternity likes to take its time, but the poet will have none of it. He sings, and singing follows Eurydice's footsteps down into the shadows. In the upper world the very air that vibrates with song is the same substance that silences it, vibration gone still, but in death there is no air—and so the dead, who can't speak but only stutter, hear a voice that rings out to the underworld's very edge. "Poetry is a form of power" is the sentence that begins Elizabeth Sewell's *The Orphic Voice*.[9] Orpheus's song filling Hades as fully as water fills a cup, as seed fills a pot, as ash fills an urn, is our primary example of lyric power. Hearing that song, those caught in infinite torment are given the miracle of temporary reprieve: Sisyphus sits on his stone; Tantalus takes a sip of water; the Danaides cease their weeping and wipe their noses.

Orpheus finds Hades and Persephone and asks what he came to ask: to bring Eurydice back to life. That's not quite the right phrase. Blanchot has it better, weirder. Orpheus does not want

> Eurydice in her daytime truth and her everyday appeal, but wants her in her nocturnal obscurity, in her distance, with her closed body and sealed face—wants to see her not when she is visible, but when she is invisible, and not as the intimacy of a familiar life, but as the foreignness of what excludes all intimacy, and wants, not to make her live, but to have living in her the plenitude of her death.[10]

Orpheus wants to bring Eurydice back into the world of day with the world of night, the other-night, intact inside her. Such might be a lyric poem's most wondrous, most fearsome desire: not to deny death, nor to reverse it, but to fold it within life itself, to say with Thales the unimaginable truth, that life and death are one. To say with Heraclitus: "The deathless are the dying, the dying are the deathless—one lives the other's death, one dies the other's life."[11] But truth in the ancient mind is also a property as weird as fate itself. It can't wholly be known but might be imagined.

So imagine—. Imagine it's true—. Hades agrees but on one condition: Orpheus cannot look back to see if Eurydice follows. So Orpheus begins again his song. Ovid gives us the words of the song he sang walking down the road to hell, but we do not get the words to the song he sings walking back up. Heraclitus says, "The road up and the road down are the same road,"[12] which is true, but I cannot imagine the song is the same. Those uphill words, we must imagine too. We must, or we might, imagine any given lyric poem, every lyric poem, is that very song. Trusting that it loves what it names, and what it names follows lovingly behind, still stunned by death's bitter work, she who we love, Eurydice. And he comes so close, Orpheus. He crosses the plains of Avernus. He feels the sun's warmth on his cheek before the sun brightens it. And just then, he looks back. Eurydice says the only word the myth gives her, "farewell." "Gloom" isn't the right word, but I don't know what the word is, into which Eurydice falls. A darkness so dark we've forgotten the word for it. Or maybe not. Maybe the word is at hand and as old as thought itself. That ancient Greek word for truth is *aletheia*, for which "truth" is a poor translation. Purer, more Orphean, would be to call *aletheia* a "not-forgetting," a "not-oblivion."

The *a-* is a privative suffix. But the root of the word is *lethe*, river of forgetting, oblivion's token, the shadow that lives within the brilliant shining forth of anything that exists so obviously that no one can deny it. It doesn't need our denial. Its oblivion is built in, as it is in us. Let us define it thus, this lyric truth, this Orphean realization: "the-shining-bright-bright-blossom-obvious-flower-of-every-every-lovely-face-face-that-like-the-morning-glory-closes-at-night-and-forgets-the-sun." What it doesn't say to us is its one word allowed? Farewell.

Farewell. It's a word that reminds me this essay should also end. Funny that one must be reminded of such things. I want to ask a simple question about Orpheus returned. With what eyes, then, does he see? On the surface of the earth, underneath the sun. Eyes that have grown accustomed to a darkness daylight can't readjust. Not wholly. One eye sees the day, and it notices, as do our eyes, that shadows seem to fall from things, a minor entity. One eye sees the night inside the day, the other-night, which notices, too, that things have shadows inside them, no minor entity but an essence. This motion is prophesized by poetry itself. Each line walks from west to east, trying to get back to morning. But each poem takes a step down as it walks farther east, so that lyric motion reveals itself as a double motion: we walk down as we walk across. Words promise us their troubled wisdom. The present tense has a little grave buried inside it. *Mnema. Sema.* What a simple thing to end up saying, and yet it must be said. A poem calls so lovingly to what it loves—a love that doesn't so much realize itself as bring what it loves into realization, as if the song could coax imagination into being. But no. Some law denies it. Some law stronger than the gods because it is stranger than the gods. So simple to say, but also I can't understand it. A poem must end. Every poem must end. What it sings of falls away, falls back. It leaves you with the desire with which you began. But, worse, it makes you desire desire itself. That you loved, that you lost. There's another poem to be written because of this mythic motion. Thank you, Orpheus. You loved, you lost, and so you love all the more. The silence of that love, love's repetition, love's reiteration. You feel you cannot speak your way into it. You need a threshold. A way to step in, to step across. Impatience builds in the mouth. This I, this I that I am, what force can be bend me back into that O that encircles silence and, in doing so, invokes the possibility of that holiest word: you. That cosmic you. That Eurydice you are. That every you is. O, you—

Circularities

A Conversation

KYLAN RICE: Today we have come together to consider the figure of
the pot in its relation to poetry—which is perhaps auspicious,
since both *poetry* and *pottery*, near homophones or homographs,
refer through their etymology to acts of bringing-together or gathering. "Pottery" may come from a word meaning "to swell," as in
the swelled-out shape of a vessel, able to contain by making space
within itself, and "poetry" may come from a proto-Indo-European
word meaning to "pile, stow, or gather," a sense prior to its origins
in the Greek word *poesis*, which means "to make." One might stow
or gather in a shirtfront, a basket, or some other kind of swelling,
containing form, like a pot. Maybe we can begin by dwelling on
this gathering gesture. Does this feel to you to be a first principle
for the poet? Making as a kind of piling, stowing, gathering?

DAN BEACHY-QUICK: What it most immediately reminds me of is that
in the Greek, the word for "speaking"—to speak, I speak—*legow,
legein*—also means to gather, as in, for example, a gathering of
acorns or the gathering of any kind of nourishing substance. So
this link between poetry and gathering, assembling, and finding
a means of containing that which has been gathered in order to
minimize waste feels deeply right to me.

It's funny to think that many of my formative experiences
as a poet have involved pots, though at the time, I hardly knew
it. When I was an undergrad, I studied Chinese art history, and
I had thought that it might be what I pursued for my career. In
many ways I felt so thrilled and at home in the kind of thinking that I found in that ancient Chinese scholarly tradition, of
the Song Dynasty tradition in particular. The woman who was
teaching that course was a curator at the Denver Art Museum

and brought the class in to let us hold these neolithic pots from Painted Pot culture, dated from around 2000 BC, if I'm remembering right. The vessels were large, meant for containing what has been assembled—seeds, but also wine, oil, or water, so they had to be made watertight. They were coiled instead of thrown on the wheel, so the potter had to put their hand inside the pot to smooth the coils and create a leakproof wall. I got to hold one of these pots, to put my hand inside its mouth. When I rubbed my fingers against the wall, I could feel the indentations of the maker's fingers, which had made that vessel worthy in the way it needed to be worthy. And that sense of having my hand present in the indentation of the absent hand was one of the moments that opened something in me to what poetry could be and the way I wanted to be apprenticed to it.

This stayed latent within me, some twenty-five years, until I started teaching a Pottery and Poetry class with the ceramicist and sculptor Del Harrow after ten years of being in conversation and collaboration with him. The class became a strange, patient, common ground to ask these questions about what a pot is and what a poem is, the difficulty of the material of each art being different but having hidden inside it strange sympathies. One of those is, I think, exactly this effort to draw a circle. It's just as John Donne put it in "A Valediction: Forbidding Mourning," a poem that's been a kind of primary awakening for me, whose primary function, despite all the brilliance of its metaphoric work, is simply to draw a circle on the page, is simply to draw a circle in the reader's mind. And that circle has, for me, come to point to those astonishing two letters Emily Dickinson wrote, one to Thomas Higginson and the other to Dr. and Mrs. J. G. Holland. In the first she defines her business: "My Business is—Circumference." A few days later in a letter written to others—which I also take as some aspect of the poet's relation to thinking: the thought is continuous, the addressee not—her "business" changes. Now her business "is to love." And a few sentences later, seeing a bird, she asks it why it sings when no one hears; the bird answers: "*My* business is to *sing*," and away the bird flies. Then the letter ends.

That particular trajectory: the business of drawing a circle makes it possible for the business of love to begin, after which the last business can begin, the business of singing once again. That threefold work feels to me a profound momentum, one that begins by drawing a circle closed, drawing a circle just (Donne), and so making a shape that is able to contain. What is contained is what is loved. What is loved is everything that is there, in there, and being in there is able to be sung. That inner space has contradictions. Love precedes song. Maybe it can be no other way. Love precedes song, and song is hard. Song is a circle, or song is what fills the circle, and all that is within it is loved, is love-able, and love furthering the possibilities of love (Keats: "More happy love! More happy, happy love!") makes song necessary all over again. Not *song*, the noun; *to sing*, the infinitive verb. To sing is strange work, and as that bird flies off, I have this sense that the circle first drawn closed is now abandoned, ruptured, or broken, no longer suffices for the loving and singing an entire life must accomplish. Singing breaks the circle, and so one must learn over and over how to sing again. To do so we must learn how to love again. That work begins with drawing a circle: a circumference, a pot, a poem. To make one good pot or one good poem is a wonderful thing. But it seems to me always, more and more intensely, just the beginning of the work.

KR: In the moment that you touched the indentations made by the fingers of the ancient potter, you say you felt a kind of call that also gave you a way to imagine the composition of poems. As I see it, the grooves on the inside of the pot serve as evidence of a making process, proof that this object was made by hand. It could be said that these marks also constitute a kind of imperfection, a roughness or unevenness where the inner surface of the work wasn't fully smoothed, thereby giving the illusion that it exists independently or autonomously, sufficient to itself. When looking at a poem, is it possible to perceive these kinds of marks of imperfection left over by the maker? When reading something by Donne or Dickinson, I don't necessarily know how to look for the traces of its making, the imperfections that preserve the shape of the poet's hand. How is it possible to discern these, to touch where the poet touched?

DBQ: I think it's incredibly hard to discern, in part because the medium of language versus the medium of clay are revelatory in radically different kinds of ways, and poetry doesn't avail itself of that haptic quality of sensing error as an immediately present, physical thing. Words are unable, or unwilling, to offer us that kind of access. It takes a very rare kind of poem, and a rare kind of reader, to be able to access those moments. I do think those generous imperfections exist in certain poems, just as powerfully as the ancient potter's fingers exist inside the pot. And maybe it's easier for us to think toward this nuanced and difficult question you're asking by staying with that primary image of the living hand inside the ancient pot, feeling the remnant, the relict, the absence still present somehow of that ancient potter's living hand that made the indentation that mine is fitted into.

I'm reminded of that line from Wallace Stevens that has meant so much to me over the years: that the "imperfect is our paradise." I also think of the homonymic echoes of pots bearing the anatomical names of the human body—lips, mouths, feet, even the "hands" of handles—that, if we put a pressure on them, gain importance here. That I'm putting my hand through the *mouth* of the pot feels to me a gesture that reading of a certain kind might also be a form of reading that is a form of grasping. This is a notion I've found in ancient Greek, a language so rife with words for various kinds of knowing. There is a word I love: λαμβάνω. It means taking, receiving, grasping but also *knowing*, and somewhere within knowing, thinking. Thinking as physical gesture, that is what makes most sense to me. Poetry feels deeply attuned to such a possibility: that to read a poem—if we can make the supposition that in some ways a poem and a pot, via the etymology you gave us, are one and the same—then to read is to reach your hand into the mouth of the poem, to read is to reach your hand into the mouth of the pot, and to have your hand on the inside of an experience that is not exactly yours and yet also not exactly not yours. That sense of having my fingers in the indentations that another hand made, in an effort to make the vessel useful, feels to me that it puts upon poetry the most human kind of pressure I would want to put on it—that the poem written by someone else has been written in order to make a vessel that is usable, that contains, as well as it possibly can, an experience that without the poem would be lost entirely—lost to time, lost to mind. That the same gesture, making of pot and making of poem, can offer me that experience as it also gives me an introduction, or initiation, into my own being in time. Which involves a sense that my hand is in the process of disappearing just as this potter's hand has disappeared. What remains is not the hand but the absence of the hand in the very thing that hand made—this makes me feel that a poem can also bear these kinds of qualities.

How you access the *error* of that is a real question—an achievement even to ask. That we are evident most truly only in such errors. It helps us surrender to the simplest facts, facts as helpless as fate, such as our individual anonymous intimacy of being a subject in the world. That is only to say, no one else is living in my body but me, just as that potter was the only one living in his or her body, just as John Keats was the only one living in his body. Somehow the error is there, that fact that we are a thing we cannot help but be. Heraclitus: "Character is fate." But character isn't personality; it's a physics. It's the fundamentally nuanced fact of being a self in the world but not an identity in the world. Nerve and synapse. A body in the world, a mind in the world that forms from the senses taking the world in. Dickinson: "The Brain is wider than the Sky." This being-there, this being-there-in-the-world, feels different to me than being a personality. It is anonymous. One more member of the old chorus. And it is where one can maybe begin to find it—that error you ask after.

I think of a poem I know we'll talk about: John Keats's "Ode on a Grecian Urn." There is that moment when the mind's work of interpreting and describing all the different scenes painted on the pot's surface suddenly alters, turns to sense, to sensing, to hearing someone's panting breath, feeling someone's fevered brow, both of which must prove to be his own. That's a moment of error in the poem. A moment where the poem's intellectual design is betrayed by the fact of the body containing that mind; that moment where suddenly the poem doesn't erase error, doesn't move away from error, doesn't try to overtly return to the work it had before been doing but fuses these things together—the fact of his own mortality in the face of a work of art, art of which he's the maker, that isn't mortal in the same way that he is, that makes an immortal claim in the midst of his mortal hands . . . that's where there the error is felt—and the appearance of that error is one of the places where one feels a miracle happen in lyrical poetry. It never fails to astound me.

KR: I love this idea that the equivalent to the indentations or grooves on the inside of that ancient Chinese pot might be the distance that opens up in Keats's poem between the made thing and the body of the maker, or the fact of being embodied. We can fit our hand inside the traces of Keats's hand by attending to this moment when the poet suddenly signals his awareness that he is here (here he is), outside the artifact, the artifact in certain respects of his own making, peripheral to it even as he describes it, perishable in a way that this form he holds is not.

With respect to the difference between being a self and being an identity or a personality, I'll just add one other thing, which is that it strikes me that when we touch the traces of a hand on the inside of a poem or pot, we're not encountering the absence of a specific person. Of course, it's possible to imagine who that making person might have been. But really what we're encountering is a maker, and less so a biological human being vested with name and history and identity. Instead of touching John Keats the man, we're coming into contact with something more anonymous: John Keats the poet.

DBQ: Poetry has given me this sense, some standard of humility and honesty—though it's taken me many years to realize, and now I only want to practice it as honestly as I can—that our most intimate self is our most anonymous one. There are very few means by which to explore the self as a form of anonymity rather than of identity. I have shied almost completely away from the idea of the lyric poem as a mode of self-expression—a thing I once thought but that has fallen apart for me in certain ways, based on the kinds of experiences we're talking about. Another poem that feels to me very present in this conversation with Keats is that famous late poem he wrote, "This Living Hand." It feels worth quoting, it's so short:

This living hand, now warm and capable
Of earnest grasping, would, if it were cold
And in the icy silence of the tomb,
So haunt thy days and chill thy dreaming nights
That thou would wish thine own heart dry of blood
So in my veins red life might stream again,
And thou be conscience-calm'd—see here it is—
I hold it towards you.[1]

In that poem is the hand for whose sake you would put your own heart's blood in it so that it might live again and in order to be less accused by its pointing at you. It does feel to me that, somewhere within the artifactual phenomenon of every made thing, a hand is pointing back at us who holds what it made. Maybe it's not pointing; sometimes it's a hand of offering or of warning. But there is some gesture of the hand embedded in any made thing that is made truly. If the space of the lyric is a unique form of consciousness, which I've also come to believe is true, where the mind and the hand meld their seemingly unique potencies, and thinking is also a kind of grasping, then something of that hand's nature is also mindful, mind-full, in the deepest sense: filled with hours and eons long past the limits of the maker's life. And part of what I've come to feel, what is also the deep mythological undergirding of this poem's power, lurks within old ideas of sacrifice—sacrifices of aversion in particular, where the sacrifice wasn't made to hero or to god, but to another human, one who has died and is in the underworld, who wants a drop of blood in order to feel and speak as if alive once again. Odysseus among the shades is one vision of what it is to be a reader of poems. The ritualistic nature of reading at its deepest level is a kind of sacrifice in this way. That return—an *anabasis*—over and over again into the same poem. I hear this echo in Thoreau's sense that the "head is an organ for burrowing." It is work that lends breath back to words that otherwise have none. Reading lends blood to words that otherwise have none. And if we're unwilling to read in such a way, if our breath, and blood, and life, and experience, and mind, aren't an offering back to the poem, then maybe we're not reading correctly.

KR: After encountering it in a class I took from you, I've since had the chance to teach "This Living Hand" in my own classes. And in conversations with students, I've found that there is something problematic or at least disturbing about this demanding, aggressive little poem with respect to the reciprocal dynamic between reader and writer that we've been discussing. Or maybe my issue with this poem is just that Keats breaks his own rule by "irritably reach[ing] after," a poetic mode or mood that he identifies as one of Coleridge's weaknesses. Keats doesn't just extend his hand to the reader; he thrusts it out, almost groping or grasping. He explicitly requests a performance of the ritual that you have suggested is somehow characteristic of every poem, even if the poem never announces this essential invitation to donate blood and breath.

It strikes me that fitting your hand into the mouth of the pot to feel the hand of the maker is a different kind of gesture than the one that Keats prescribes in his poem. As students, we reach into the mouth of the pot or poem of our own volition, whereas the hand in Keats's poem compels and forces. It seems worthwhile to point out the phenomenological differences between reading Keats's poem and what it must have been like to touch the inside of the ancient pot.

DBQ: Maybe "This Living Hand," which is troubling in the way that you say it's troubling, is so in part because it breaks one of Keats's greatest gifts—his passionate ambivalence, his ability of staying appropriately in between, in those spaces of unknowing, or half knowing, and yields to an angry enervation, a fury of helplessness. But given the extreme point at which he wrote it, recognizing the approach of his own mortality, it might make sense. And if I'm remembering correctly, he was also collaborating at the time of composition with Charles Brown on the drama "Otho the Great," writing this short lyric as an aside while they were working, so something of that drama fills the poem. It's a strange, startled lyric, emerging out from a different sort of thinking, and Keats had the wisdom to write it down. But to get closer to your question, I think the pot offers an invitation where the one who holds it must act, must reach inside. It's obvious to say, but true, that the pot cannot reach into its own mouth. The nature of the pot as a made thing has been inverted in this poem. It is as if the pot suddenly has a hand coming out of it, insinuating that you're the pot, that you're the vessel, that you're the poem. It's a reversal that startles and troubles, in large part, because it undermines the unspoken but tacit relationship between reader and poem, that nearly unconscious choice where your surrender to the world of the poem is reversed, and a force is put upon you, a force that reads you, makes an object of you, puts you in the position of the art piece rather than simply the one encountering it, who can leave that encounter whenever you wish to do so. That's dizzying and strange. It can feel wildly inappropriate. But given the extremity of a life being on the edge of its livingness from which "This Living Hand" was written, it feels strangely just—a reminder of what we would rather not know, the brute fact of the body when the spirit leaves it, and the ghost voice that lurks in anything once alive, demands life again. Most poems ask less—just a breath. But this poem asks for blood. Asks how it is we can dare to live when the poet no longer does. That is an awful question, but I don't think it's unfair.

KR: This startling image of a hand reaching out of an urn makes me think about the relationship between the body and the pot or the poem. One feature of the pot, cup, or vase (as distinct from the vat, the tun, or the tub) is that it is fitted to the human body; it is made with reference to the lip and the hand, to the strength of the back and the arms, to the flat of the top of the head. It is designed with portability in mind, made to be lifted, carried, and set down. In the case of the urn, it is made to hold the human body after it has been reduced to ashes: that which you held eventually holds you.

In your work, the pot frequently appears as a funerary urn,
sometimes with reference to Keats's Grecian urn or Thomas
Browne's *Urn Burial*. Yet, it is also an object associated with life,
with eating and especially drinking, bypassing the cupped hand to
sip, savor, and store or save for later, to extend the time of enjoyment. Can you talk about this paradox, the pot as a keeper of the
remains of the dead as well as a tool, not just for sustaining life
but also for extending the time of enjoyment? How can we have
this deathliness in the pot as well as this vitality? Is this duality
true of poems as well?

DBQ: You ask a complicated and beautiful question. It's a question
I feel that only now I'm deeply in the midst of discovering, a
question I feel like I'm living in and writing toward, am writing
in hopes of discovering, so I fear my answer will be less coherent
than is ideal.

But I might begin back with Keats's urn. Because just as you
say, I do feel that eventually every such vessel in my poems
becomes an urn of a kind. And I think it is so because I feel caught
in a strange and primary irony that I suspect poetry is also our
introduction to, and the fundament of that irony is what Keats
discovers in "Ode on a Grecian Urn": that there is no way to get
to the inside of the pot until one has died, until the pot contains
oneself, and in some awful and full-of-awe manner the inside of
the pot—the silence on the inside of the pot, the usefulness of the
inside of the pot—that is a thing, in some phenomenal, factual,
fated way, denied the one who makes it. Bringing the thought to
poems, there is this astonishing difficulty that at times feels cruel
to me in the way that fate can feel cruel, or a joke can feel cruel
(and we should remember that the gods tend to laugh at fate,
feeling so implicated by it): sometimes it feels humanly inevitable
that the only time one is inside the vessel of the poem, the made
thing of the poem, is in the writing of it. And then somehow
there's no way back in, or that the work of poetry puts the poet in
this wholly irreconcilable condition, where one is inside a thing
out of which there is no way to escape, and outside of the same
thing, and at the same time that there is no way to enter—and this
division of maker and made, the maker of the thing and the thing

the maker's made, the way a poem divorces us from what we have written in order to keep itself whole. . . . This is mystifying and painful to me.

If the primary gesture of a poem is, as Dickinson suggests, the making of circumference, we might ask what that circumference does. It makes against an absolute blankness something that says, "The blankness inside this shape is a different blankness than the blankness outside it." One is a blankness or emptiness that is of use—a kind of chaos turned cosmos, given cosmic possibilities, and the other is just chaos entire. The trouble with poetry as I've come to be troubled by it is that, in making, you put yourself on the outside of the things that you want to contain and sing of and, by that singing, learn to love. For poets who tend to be prolific (of which, I suppose, I'm one), the conditions of that prolific being is completely shattered by this irony: that there is no other way to be inside the poem save by making the next poem, making the next pot, even though all that work does is deepen the crisis that has created the desperate necessity of making a poem.

And I feel this thought echoed in ways that I could not have suspected. I've been translating pre-Socratic philosophy, thinking much about Anaxagoras, who says that the whole of the universe is governed by *nous*, governed by Mind, and mind is at work on atomically small particles that can be assembled into all the varied appearances of the material world. But that Mind is wholly separate. Mind is not able to take part in the things that it shapes, and so the mind, the hands, all of it in the end feels to me so worrisomely and anxiously outside, outside the thing that it's made. I have this fear that we're not included. And I get that fear from Keats.

KR: And yet it strikes me that being on the outside, the worrisome fact of being unincluded, is precisely where life might be said to exist. Based on what you've just described—this feeling of urgency or anxiety upon discovering yourself outside the pot or poem, holding it in your living hands as you form it, breathing above it, panting after it, to be inside of it perhaps—it seems to me that when you create an object from which you are excluded, you are returned to life, since (as you observe) if you were inside the pot, the made thing, you would be ashes.

DBQ: We should fill out the other side of the extreme I all-too-typically take us toward, the one you're pointing out so beautifully, and which is also inside the question you asked. When we think about the objects among which we spend most of time, the objects we spend our lives among (and here we hear Oppen quoting Maritain: "We spend our lives among objects / and to see them / is to know ourselves"), that we share names with them—–lips, feet, arms, back—there's an intimate linguistic connection between our life and the things we live our life among, almost every one of which will outlive our particular life. There's a strange kind of companionship that objects can offer, including the kind of object a poem is. And one of the things that feels to me truly kind about poetry—and we should keep in mind that Keats himself talked about poetry as a friend to humankind much earlier in his poetry and in the great Odes, but it's there, it's there in the "Grecian Urn" actually, and elsewhere—is that it does allow us to keep at hand experiences that would otherwise leave and leave hardly a trace. The art object, the poem, it creates a delay—the very word Marcel Duchamp used to describe his later work: "a delay in glass." Without the delay that puts experience—of thought, of supposition, of hazardous leap into faith, of doubt—into form, without that graciousness, without that happiness, we might simply lose those aspects of ourselves that refuse to be tamed into the rote procedures of day-to-day. In great poetry that generosity can condense down to the instantaneous distraction of the senses that obliterates the poem's concentration: those gnats in Keats's "To Autumn." That he hears them and, hearing them, hears the twitter of the swallows. Such delay is the grace of realizing that everything is allowed to be included and can be, if one is attuned and at work in honest and humble ways. It's a beautiful thing that keeps alive the "isolated verisimilitude" of open experience long past the experience that should be ours. That feels to me one of our most human beauties, one of our most humane kinds of beauty. To put it in simpler terms, and to return us to the source of your question, there is simply the honorable beauty of holding a pot, of filling a cup, of making a poem.

KR: As much as we've been contemplating similarities between two forms, the pot and the poem, I've also been wondering about their differences. Fundamentally, it seems to me we might need a pot more than we need a poem insofar as we need to store, to drink. I would hazard to guess that a certain kind of poetry, or maybe even poetry in general, emerged anciently out of the social form of the drinking circle, the circle where we're gathered together and telling stories and singing songs and maybe even creating a song as the cup is passed from person to person, taking turns to develop it further. It strikes me that if there weren't cups to pass from person to person in the drinking circle, there might not be poems. Where would poems be without pots or cups?

This is related, perhaps, to your sense of the humanity of the poem and my sense of the vitality it helps foster by excluding the poet. Again, I think there is a way in which the poem as an urn, as an object that carries death or an intimation of death, is able to also bring our attention in unexpected ways to everything that is outside of it. I think of Stevens's "Anecdote of the Jar," for example. As I read it, this poem is about an empty jar on a hill in Tennessee that manages to contain or admit an image of the world as an effect of the transmission of light through glass. By being empty, it refracts the world in all of its color and life, including the lives of those to whom we pass the cup, who sit beside us in the drinking circle.

DBQ: There's so much in what you're saying. First, that idea of song developing anciently, of people sitting in a circle and handing a different kind of circle around; in some ways, as the oral tradition contained within epic and lyric poetry might make us guess, those sitting in that circle gather words from one another and further them, speaking as I suppose language always speaks within us (though we seldom pause and recognize it), that we speak for ourselves in words that aren't our own, that many mouths speak from our mouths. That intricate nesting of circles within circles feels real to me, feels right.

I want to get to the Stevens poem, but there are a couple of things on my mind, since you brought it up in light of jars and pots and poems and jugs—all such vessels. One of the difficult things that poetry—or maybe it's poetry of a certain kind—might make us hazard is a guess that a thought, idea, feeling, or perception makes a claim toward reality, makes a claim that is just as real, just as profoundly actual, as is a table, a hammer, a cup, any tangible object. A poem somehow holds something as real and essential as water, as seeds, as air, as fire and earth and makes this elemental being something available to us. It's a thought that requires us to think, as Gottlieb Frege put it, that there is a "fourth dimension"—one in which a thought is as real as a hammer is real but real in a different way. And maybe it could be, in the lovely way you're imagining anciently back to the kind of gathering a poem might emerge from, that some vestige of another's experience gets to be yours without your having had to live that experience. The myriad ways in which a great poem enters you and empties you (to go back to your etymology of the pot as a swelling that makes you more capacious) feels to me a potent thought, if that emptiness means you become more capable of the openness required for living a decent life, a life lived more fully because it is a life that can contain more more honestly.

I think Stevens's "Anecdote of the Jar" enters into this conversation in a curious way. It's begun to strike me as a poem that is the opposite side of the same fact of Keats's poem—that the jar is transparent where the urn is opaque, decorated or painted with different scenes. The jar is abandoned on a hillside; the urn is held, touched, turned. . . . Curiously, and in a strange way counter to the story you told to guide our thinking toward the "Anecdote of the Jar," that jar in Tennessee exists wholly outside the social realm—save the language that shows it to us. It is a thing placed with purpose and then abandoned; the human element leaves, and the world in all its wordly wildness gathers around a jar that is unable to take part in that world, that wildness. There is something of that deep paradox, the irony of being inside of that jar and outside of it at the same time, never both at once, that we've often spoken of—this fear that the poem is a kind of hut one is within and unable to leave and exactly at the same time, outside of, and unable to enter. It is a version of the moment in Simone Weil when she speaks of the walls in a prison, the walls that prisoners in the cells knock upon to communicate with one another, a separation that is also a link. One is in the jar and not in it—both are true. Such is the weird fate consciousness might be—an irreconcilable condition. I find this in Stevens's poem, which maybe here we should hear:

I placed a jar in Tennessee,
And round it was, upon a hill.
It made the slovenly wilderness
Surround that hill.

The wilderness rose up to it,
And sprawled around, no longer wild.
The jar was round upon the ground
And tall and of a port in air.

It took dominion everywhere.
The jar was gray and bare.
It did not give of bird or bush,
Like nothing else in Tennessee.[2]

The jar is also a pivot around which the wildness of the world grows outside of any foreordained order. The old story sung around the old circle repeats itself: chaos and cosmos. If the jar were different, if it maintained its human capacity, if it stayed within any possibility of the social realm, the realm of civilization, it wouldn't be "slovenly" enough. If it were, so to say, still held in human hands—as Keats's urn is—it wouldn't be a slovenly wilderness but a wildness that also nurtures, furthers, ushers us deeper into life. Some aesthetic and ethical claim is being made—maybe "claim" is too strong a word. . . . Some aesthetic and ethical portrait, or picture, or description, or image is being given to us by Stevens, and it is a contradiction that doesn't reconcile itself: a jar which is meant to carry fruit preserves is never filled, is never put to its human and worldly use, and its eternal emptiness is against the world and shows us what a well-made thing ill-used might bring us to. It breeds a chaos it cannot be part of. And that feels [like] an indictment of those other jars we are always making and abandoning and hoping the world fills them . . . the heart, the mind.

KR: I want to focus more deeply on the idea of emptiness or hollowness of both jar or pot and poem, since I think this idea is central to your poetics. And I think this might bring us back to the circle, too, which holds in itself a blankness that is distinct from external blankness in that it is usable.

In an essay from *Of Silence and Song*, you refer briefly to "the circle of the urn itself." I know that the form of the circle is of special importance to you, having written *Circle's Apprentice*, which takes for its epigraph a quote from Ralph Waldo Emerson: "Our life is an apprenticeship to the truth, that around every circle another can be drawn; that there is no end in nature, but every end is a beginning; that there is always another dawn risen on mid-noon, and under every deep a lower deep opens."

If the circle is an urn, it seems to me that it is saturated with dimension, a form that emerges in space as a result of circling, or being spun on the potter's wheel. Circling (with the hand in the mouth of the forming pot) produces this swelling out, this rondure, space to be filled. Just as infinity is hard to think about, there is something frustrating or at least literally unfulfilling in Emerson's claim that there "is no end in nature." But perhaps frustration as a result of circling, and the feeling of emptiness or unfulfillment that this involves, can be said to give rise to forms of holding, retention. Does this seem right to you? Is there a relationship between circles or circling and emptiness? And is there also a relationship between emptiness and holding? If so, what does this look like in practice, your practice? How do we pass through the void of the circle to obtain powers of retention?

DBQ: For a long time, I've felt at the bedrock level that something in the nature of the urge and the urgency toward making a work of art—be it poem, be it pot, whatever form it might be—resides in the replication of the primordial processes by which existence came to be. At that dark, anonymous depth in which poems might be written—where putting a word on a blank page makes a kind of circle, that circumference of Dickinson's we've spoken about—that gesture is a participation in (because it's a recovery of) the very powers by which we explain to ourselves the possibility of our own being something rather than nothing. I think that's what the "business of circumference" eventually means. It understands that all of us are pressed against some existential blank that should, by all rights and purposes, make null the possibility of our life: a kind of infinite blankness evermore blank. One can imagine suddenly how the universe is pictured for us—an infinite expansion. But expansion into what? It's a paradox that breaks the mind with its utter simplicity. A question of the pre-Socratics, of Aristotle, of Dickinson (again) herself: "Unto the Whole—how Add?" The universe itself seems a curious proof of Emerson's claim in "Circles," drawing eternally a next circle around itself, center nowhere and everywhere. But those circles, that circling, thinking even of the Sufi leftward spin toward the heart, is for me a kind of sacred ritual that brings me back to what Stevens pursued his whole poetic career: that one bears a responsibility to the wondrous verb *is*. To make a poem is to conduct an experiment inside the possibility of being, not by saying what being is but by making the shape in which being becomes possible. For me that shape is just a circle, a circle made just—and what that circle circles is an emptiness that suddenly becomes rife with cosmic possibility, that promises where chaos had been, order is possible. In some way the circle is also the circle of adornment: the pendant on a necklace, an earring, a pearl. A poem feels to me an adornment on invisible forces and patterns we cannot see save for the adornment—no earlobe without the earring, no orbit without the moon. But these invisible patterns govern our lives. We have no access to it but to adorn it. Something strange and deep inside our nature occurs when we allow ourselves to make a circle.

Paradox abounds on the potter's wheel—for instance, centering as a motion that stands still. And there is the difficulty of raising the wall, widening the volume, where any distortion in that spinning stillness threatens to destroy the whole vessel. But that clay wall between thumb and fingers also describes principles one could think of as cosmic. How to trace the hand against the material in such a way that the result is more emptiness, more useful emptiness, for the pot can contain more. There is in the work some experiment in Emerson's sense of reciprocity as the primary law of the universe. How matter in motion responds to a force not in motion—the seeming stillness of the potter's hand. It's hard, maybe impossible to discern, but the work of a poem feels similar. As with the potter's wheel, it combines opposites— the passive and the active. I keep thinking of the strange passivity of the clay—it responds to every force we put to it, but spinning, the potter's hand is passively responding to the nature of the clay. Some fine balance between action and reception is profoundly in play, something I hear in Keats's letter where he speaks of a "diligent indolence," something I find in ancient Greek, its "middle voice," where the action the verb performs itself against itself, and where certain words change their meaning in stunning ways: where the verb of poetry itself, *poieow*, "to do, to make," becomes *poiesthai*, "to consider." The poem must be made before its thought can be thought. The pot must be made before it can contain what it contains. That creation of emptiness that is the throwing of a pot parallels the hidden emptiness we make when we make a poem. The emptiness of Dickinson's circle. This beautiful question: What can the poem contain? And how profoundly it alters how we might imagine a poem, that feels always so full of the thing it is. That the words, the lines, just mark a boundary, a wall, and nothing more. To be able to think that the poem is a form of emptiness—this is what I worry about now. What I try to teach. That the lifelong practice of making poems is also the lifelong practice of making yourself ever more empty—that what poetry does is create more emptiness inside us. I obviously don't mean that in a pejorative way. I mean that reading poems, writing poems, those co-creative activities, the gathering of all that's gathered in order to make a poem whatever it is a poem is—to go back to the germ from which our whole conversation has sprung—is a kind of swelling, the swelling a larger form of gathering needs. You spend a life getting more empty exactly so you can hold more life. Poetry might be this practice: around the circle you've drawn, to draw a larger circle. To be apprentice to the circle.

KR: This notion of the hidden emptiness we make when we make a poem seems key to me, as well as your suggestion earlier that the poem is a circle inscribing a blankness or an emptiness on the page that demarcates a usable blank from a universal blank. At first it might seem obvious: a poem can't be written unless a page is blank. Or again, a poem can't be spoken unless there is silence, a preliminary inhalation of breath. But, as you've intimated, it seems to me that in your work there is an even more profound connection between poem and void.

It's almost as if your work concerns itself with what it might mean for silence to speak itself, or for the words of a poem to somehow illuminate or reproduce the blankness of the page—to become blanker than the page, even readier in its blankness for new writing. I'll just note that there is a strange kind of comfort or tidiness or symmetry in this kind of thinking. If a poem successfully apologizes for its own existence by attempting to become indistinguishable from the nothingness that is prior to it, then it manages to foreclose any challenge or contest to its reason for being. It doesn't have to explain why there is something rather than nothing, simply pointing back to the nothingness from which it came, identifying with it. "The medium [becomes] the message," as the media theorist Marshall McLuhan claimed. In this case, the message is nothingness, a condition that the poem devoutly wishes to restore.

And yet, in practice it seems to me impossible for any poem to unspeak itself or unmake itself, to speak silence or even to adequately honor the silence from which it came. We are always left with an indefensible residuum, some excess or dross produced in the creative process that inheres in the poem itself.

DBQ: Walking home from teaching workshop just the other day, feeling again this conflict my students so often feel, wanting the poem to be a marker of their identity, their actual individual existence, and my insistent suggestion that a poem is also other than a means of self-expression or even an expression of a self, I felt the problem articulate itself in me anew: that one wants a poem to sing of the vitality of one's being, but one also wants the poem to sing Being's vitality. But maybe I should begin again, all too typically in an ancient mode. This idea of apology feels potent to me. I think I have the nature of an apologist. Before I speak about anything meaningful, I feel I should apologize. For a long time that instinct felt to me like the opposite side of an arrogance that self-deprecation probably is, but I've come to understand that instinct differently—as wanting to offer in words something that simultaneously works against words, an *apo*, a motion against *logos*. I've thought what I want to offer isn't an *apo* but an *upo*, an *upology*, a kind of speaking that occurs underneath the words I speak. Both give figure of something dear to me: to speak and not speak simultaneously is somehow to me the most potent work a poet can do. And, as is the case with potent, poetic work, it is also an impossible one. How to be at work inside that impossibility has been my longest ongoing question, a question asking itself in me since I began writing poems, unconsciously for most of my life, and now quite consciously. I think often of Stesichorus's "Palinode." He'd written a poem blaming Helen for the Trojan War, in that long tradition of blaming Helen, and by Helen was made blind, because the story wasn't true—she never was at Troy. So Stesichorus writes another poem, a palinode in apology to the error his previous poem had made, and once the apology is made, he's given back his sight. That small story has become for me a template of what poetic work might be—not that the poem I write after having written a poem furthers the earlier but undermines it, *apo*logizes or *upo*logizes for it, begins anew, but anew in a place the earlier poem cleared. It is as if each next poem is trying to recover or reclaim the primordial blankness lying underneath any form of life—one that is deeper, truer, more availing of creative nature than the previous poem could be. So there is this sense, an impossible one, that I'm always trying to write the first poem I've ever written. I can imagine every poem I've ever written as a palinode, unsinging what I sung before, in order to sing more truly, more honestly—and if I might be bluntly honest about it—with the same hopes that Stesichorus had: to no longer be blind. Somehow I've been blind my whole life; and I want to learn how to see. The only way that I can come to that sight is by writing a poem that is also an apology and that tries to apologize truly for the error it's made. But there's a fundamental trouble. Unlike Stesichorus, I don't know what lie it is I've told. And it seems like I can see, even if I can't. It's only in the space of the page where lyric consciousness reigns that I realize the errors of my ways. I sense something of the assumptions I've made and operated by, and I have a desire to get rid of those, as much as I possibly can, and the only tool I know I have is the poem, and the words make up a poem.

That leads me to another kind of sense, one I worry is more mystical than philosophical. It's a strange way to think about poetry, but it is how I think about it: I want most to understand poetry as a vessel that preserves the silence out of which it emerges and, in doing so, makes it more silent—that is to say, the drawing of a circle, the business of making a circumference, makes a usable emptiness. Every word of the poem is beholden to an unguessable purpose: every word must sing itself around the silence it preserves within it. To read the poems puts your hand around that silence, as your hand might fit around a cup. A silence that can be held in no other way.

KR: But it also strikes me that the poem needs to fail to contain or preserve that silence, which is manifestly *not it*. A poem is a breaking of silence, irreparable—just as singing is the breaking of a circle, as you earlier suggested. It tries to preserve silence by shattering it and then always fails to approach that breathless origin, receding from it exponentially the more it tries to speak the opposite of speech. Truer to me than a poem that works to cancel itself by working toward silence is the messy dross of that process. Noise is the outcome of all of those attempts to articulate or hold silence—not just the noise of the poem but also the noise of the life that writes, the noise of the world that surrounds and gets refracted by the glass that forms the empty jar in Tennessee. In the attempt to preserve silence, the world rushes in. This is the next, harder accomplishment: to let the "warm love in," as Keats puts it in "Ode to Psyche." To let the world flow in, after building this primary relationship between poem and void or poem and silence, living in the aftermath of an impossible silence.

DBQ: You make me realize that if somehow the idea of an original blank could suffice, that even the cave walls of Lascaux would be blank still. But that idea of an ur-blankness leaves us blank too. Those cave walls are wondrously not blank. Bison. Horses. Bird-headed men holding spears, holding staffs. Those silhouettes of hands. I think of them often, the strange lesson of them. I realize that our first image of ourselves isn't our face—to which we have no access; I cannot see my face, I can only see out of it—but our hands. It makes a primordial sense to me that our first self-portraits would be of our hands, of blowing a kind of ink against the hand and leaving behind its absence. To see ourselves in that absence has some echo of the silence we're speaking about, that we first learn to see ourselves by making a blankness whose outline defines us. There is a work inside blankness and against it, a work inside silence and against it, that in working against each preserves the possibility of both. An image, a word. What you sense so truly is that we begin the work by betraying its goal. We speak, we sing. I think this is why Keats's Odes so often begin with a sense of trespass, with an apology for secret or silence broken: "Thou still unravished bride of quietness," saying which is silence's ravishment. What is so continually shocking to me inside Keats's "Ode on a Grecian Urn," a poem that has come to mean more to me in some ways than any other poem, is that the poem is also preserving what must be protected even from us. The poem is preserving something so astonishingly sacred and holy and necessary that even we who make the poem are a threat to it. And that courage of the poem, that insane unthinkable work of preserving some silence out of which everything emerges is again just . . . unspeakable. It shatters me into what feels a proper humility.

KR: Much of what we've been discussing is, I think, illustrated by your poem "Moon Jar Canto," and I think it may be worthwhile to spend some time dwelling with it.

MOON JAR CANTO (XII)

*] the full moon is two half-moons joined
the old word for such a joint is harmony
harmony joins the two halves of the moon together
and makes the moon whole [ ] there's a lot of emptiness
inside the moon the moon is made of this emptiness
and it is glazed a blinding white eyeless as the open
eyes of gods when hearing a heart beat
they open their eyes on the animal they hunt [ ] some
times they hunt the moon and sometimes
the moon is the hunter [ ] the moon
has a heart and that heart thinks and pulses
and I who am saying I with you as you say I
am an echo of that pulse or am I a thought
that is the moon's thought*

*( )
life borrows light borrows life
I like the riddle even if I have no choice but to be it [ ] or
so I sometimes think [ ] building so much by hand
building the moon by hand
building by hand my hands and building these thoughts [ ] my
head is feet and hands [ ] the moon has a foot and a lip
and when the harmony limps or lisps
the moon needs a dark crutch to stay full and bright [ ] some
times the moon is a bow drawn back
sometimes it's the string of the lyre [ ] some
times the moon is a pot filled with smaller moons
rings and earrings and some other singing that has no name*

but adorns the emptiness [ ] adores and
adorns the emptiness as it grows inside us [

While it feels to me that anything I could say about "Moon Jar Canto" has already been said in the course of our conversation, one way to begin talking about it would be to observe that, formally, the poem is written in two halves or parts, and the second part is kind of a gloss or commentary on the activity described in the first. In particular, the sixteenth line—"I like the riddle even if I have no choice but to be it"—seems to signal that what has come before it is a kind of riddle or riddling of the poem by itself. The riddle that this poem *is* is a fated condition: "I have no choice but to be it." This fate is a function of a particular process of composition or of making, which this poem dramatizes in the first stanza and then discusses in the second. To think about this fated process, I recall a lesson that I learned from you along the way, which is that a poem listens to itself. In other words, one effective method of composition is for a poem to reflect or redound upon itself, each line an apprentice to the line it follows, in much the same way as Emerson is apprentice to circles upon circles, deeps that open up to lower deeps. When composing a poem, the first line is the seed, the genetic material for the poem that unfolds as a ramification of all of the manifold consequences and deviations that its initial, initiatory gesture implies. In "Moon Jar Canto," it seems that the first half draws a series of circles, and then that second half reflects on and extends this drawing, so that the poem enacts the discovery of a riddle produced in commitment to immanence or immanent emergence as a mode of composition.

DBQ: Reading this poem after our conversation does feel a little uncanny—simply to see how much of the concerns and ways of thinking toward poetry that we've discussed are embedded inside this strange poem that, as you say, is constructed of two halves. Each half is meant to be one half of the two pots that, put together, create these astonishing moon jars, a very old form of Korean ceramics that I have come to love and feel a certain obsession toward.

I do think in the end Keats is at the heart of that line, "I like the

riddle even if I have no choice but to be it"—by which I've come
to understand that a poem is meant to give us to the riddle, put
us in the maze, make of us a labyrinth, not to get out of it or to
solve it but to finally understand the complexity that we're in and
that we are. Maybe this is why poetry has such a long history of
being a frustration to philosophers: it's not interested in the end
in solving a problem but in offering a problem—not interested
in solving difficulty but in letting difficulty claim us, and that's a
hard position to be in but a truthful one.

KR: Returning to my earlier sense that a first line is a circle that ripples
or ramifies, it seems to me that a first line or first initiating movement provides the poem with every twist or turn it might contain
and that it is the job of the poet to pursue each of those paths, not
in order to exit the labyrinth, as you say, but instead to get a fuller
sense of the labyrinth as a form or pattern worthy of consideration
in itself. Finding a way out in the disappearance of every way out
is one way for a poem to exist and, in doing so, to make of itself a
kind of fate, a reason for being.

Just so, your poem does not take for granted the fact of its own
existence. This poem tries to apologize for itself by accounting for
everything involved in its creation, including the creator itself:
"I like the riddle even if I have no choice but to be it [ ] or / so
I sometimes think [ ] building so much by hand / building the
moon by hand / building by hand my hands." Here, you grapple
with the fact that something exists on the page at all. And the
hand that writes doesn't just build a poem—it also has to build
itself in the process. Everything here emerges out of itself, in
the midst or middle of itself, self-mediating, the poet and poem
co-constructing each other, appearing out of nothing, the nothingness of the blank page, trying to figure out what "harmony"
or song might be possible under such conditions. In this poem,
nothing sings nothing, tries to harmonize with itself.

What results is not so much harmony as a "dark crutch." Self-
harmonizing inevitably "limps," "lisps," or falters. And that limp
or lisp, that dark crutch, takes us back to my sense of the dross or
excess that forms around the poem as it tries to cancel itself out or

as it tries to redeem the silence that was prior to it. There's a kind of hobbling or awkwardness, an awkward, panting life, that we are given as a consequence of every poem, figured here as a lisp or a limp, an imperfection, or as figured earlier as grooves or indentations on the inside of an ancient pot.

DBQ: There's much I want to say in what you bring up. If we take that Emersonian idea, that "law of reciprocity" we talked about earlier—and if we suppose, as I think poetry invites us to do, that it *is* the primary fact of the world and that poems offer themselves as sites of such experiments—then it seems to me that just because you can say "I" outside of the poem in one's daily life, you shouldn't assume that this gives you permission to say "I" inside the poem. And by that I mean that somehow one of the strange reciprocities, or *harmonies* as it's spoken of in this poem (in which a harmony is that reciprocal form of jointure, dovetailing, a drawing into proper tension) that if a poem is going to say "I," as this poem eventually does, that it must build into itself the possibility of that "I" uttering itself as an "I," as a pronoun, as a first person. I get this sense that everything that is in a poem has to be built by hand inside that poem, and nothing can be assumed that it fits inside simply because in 99.5 percent of my life everything that is needed is more or less at hand. The poem must make available what is at hand, which I hear as exactly what you were talking about in the nature of a first line—a sense I very much share. Just this morning I was reading a review in the *New York Times* that is organized around the thought that the poet's search for the next line is so hard because everything is available, that there's this absolute freedom, and you can say anything you will yourself to say (Elisa Gabbert, "The Lyric Decision: How Poets Figure Out What Comes Next"). I read that and thought, that's not it, not at all. What's so hard about writing the next line of the poem is exactly the opposite problem. It's that somehow that next line has already been written simply by the advent of the previous one existing. Some fate filters down into the poem that is a radical limit on the possibilities of where that poem can go. The poet who gets to the blankness of the next line and feels that anything can still be written is available isn't a poet that I can wholly understand. That exertion of self, exertion of will, exertion of intelligence, bewilders me to some degree. It's a freedom that takes pleasure in all of the things I come to poetry to dismantle in myself. Most of my poetry practice is writing a line and then working not too quickly to write the next one. I work on not-writing far more than I work on writing. I want to let the possibility of the next line to unfold not from my intelligence but from the poem's. I don't know how to do that except by waiting until I hear the possibility of a line that seems inevitably to emerge from what that first line has made possible. I feel like I'm practicing, and you're practicing, and a number of us are practicing, an art of an occult and different nature—a very ancient art inside a very contemporary world. And it's curious to watch that particular position play itself out.

KR: As we talk, I'm made to think of a line from Robert Duncan's "The Structure of Rime (I)" in which the poet writes that "writing is first a search in obedience." Although, I would add something here: as we apprentice ourselves to the first line of a poem, working to obey whatever fate it augurs, I think it's important that the truth of that fate is never quite grasped as we proceed from one line to the next. Instead, a stumbling ensues. When I heed that first line and try to be obedient to it, I inevitably disobey. Inevitably I limp to the next line and the next, which only approximates whatever fate was available in the line prior to it. In my practice at least, the poem digresses or divagates from itself even as it tries to be true to itself. It hobbles along on a dark crutch, the crutch of accident, the falling shy of skill or cleverness, so that something like the world rushes in where the poet's hand slips.

DBQ: I want to just note that you've done a quite extraordinary thing: very beautifully you have answered your own question by which you started out our conversation, which is, How do we have access to the nature of such error? We do so exactly by the process you just described, in which the first line posits a kind of fate that is the poem's truest form, and line by line—even in trying to listen, even in trying to heed and explore that fate—we err in doing so. So, strangely, line by line by line of a poem is both fate's inevitable forward step and the palinode's backward apology, trying to begin again: the riddle of experience that does and undoes itself in equal measure. A line tries to correct, to re-true itself to the error the previous line made against that fate, and then continues the error, because there is no other way. The beauty of a poem's particular idiosyncrasy is that it limps its way through the fate of what the ideal poem could be, or should be—the poem that we could never write.

Notes

The Hut of Poetry

1. Kabir, *The Bijak of Kabir*, trans. Linda Hess and Shukedeo Singh (Oxford: Oxford University Press, 2002), 56.

2. Kabir, *Bijak of Kabir*, 49.

3. Kabir, *Bijak of Kabir*, 41.

4. Mircea Eliade, *Rites and Symbols of Initiation: The Mysteries of Birth and Rebirth*, trans. Willard R. Trask (Woodstock, CT: Spring Publications, 1995), x.

5. Eliade, *Rites and Symbols of Initiation*, 34.

6. Emily Dickinson, *The Poems of Emily Dickinson*, ed. R. W. Franklin (Cambridge, MA: Belknap Press, 1999), 152–53.

7. Emily Dickinson, *Letters of Emily Dickinson*, ed. Mabel Loomis Todd (Boston: Roberts Brothers, 1894), 315.

8. Walt Whitman, *Leaves of Grass* (Boston: Small, Maynard, 1904), 34.

9. John Keats, *Keats: Poems Published in 1820*, ed. M. Robertson (Oxford: Clarendon Press, 1909), 198–99.

Arcadian Survey

1. Robert Duncan, *Selected Poems*, ed. Robert J. Bertholf (New York: New Directions, 1997), 54.

2. Daniel Heller-Roazen, *Echolalias* (Cambridge, MA: Zone Books, 2005), 160.

3. John Keats, *Selected Letters of John Keats*, ed. Grant F. Scott (Cambridge, MA: Belknap Press, 2002), 92–93.

4. Sappho, *If Not, Winter*, trans. Anne Carson (New York: Knopf Doubleday, 2009), 215.

As in the Green Trees

1. John Keats, *Complete Poems*, ed. Jack Stillinger (Cambridge, MA: Harvard University Press, 1991), 479.

2. William Blake, *Selected Poems*, ed. Nicholas Shrimpton (Oxford: Oxford University Press, 2019), 59.

Of Time and Timelessness in the Poetic Sentence

1. Saint Augustine, *The Confessions*, trans. R. S. Pine-Coffin (New York: Penguin Classics, 1961), 25.

2. Saint Augustine, *The Confessions*, 29.

3. Saint Augustine, *The Confessions*, 209.

4. Saint Augustine, *The Confessions*, 215.

5. Marcel Proust, *In the Shadows of Young Girls in Flower*, trans. James Grieve (New York: Penguin Classics, 2004), 379–80.

To Arrive in Zeno's Thought

1. Peter Gizzi, "A Panic That Can Still Come Upon Me," *The Outernationale* (Middletown, CT: Wesleyan University Press, 2008), 2.

2. Gizzi, "A Panic That Can Still Come Upon Me," 1.

3. Ralph Waldo Emerson, *Emerson's Essays, "Experience"* (New York: Harper Perennial, 1981), 292–323.

4. Gizzi, "A Panic That Can Still Come Upon Me," 1.

5. Gizzi, "A Panic That Can Still Come Upon Me," 2.

6. Gizzi, "A Panic That Can Still Come Upon Me," 1.

7. Gizzi, "A Panic That Can Still Come Upon Me," 4–5.

8. Gizzi, "A Panic That Can Still Come Upon Me," 2, 3.

9. Robert Edward Duncan, *The Truth and Life of Myth: An Essay in Essential Autobiography* (Fremont, MI: Sumac Press, 1968), 13.

10. Gizzi, "A Panic That Can Still Come Upon Me," 6.

11. Gizzi, "A Panic That Can Still Come Upon Me," 1.

12. Duncan, *Truth and Life of Myth*, 23.

13. Gizzi, "A Panic That Can Still Come Upon Me," 7.

14. Duncan, *Truth and Life of Myth*, 13.

15. Gizzi, "A Panic That Can Still Come Upon Me," 7.

16. Gizzi, "A Panic That Can Still Come Upon Me," 7.

17. Gizzi, "A Panic That Can Still Come Upon Me," 9.

18. Gizzi, "A Panic That Can Still Come Upon Me," 9.

19. Gizzi, "A Panic That Can Still Come Upon Me," 9.

20. Gizzi, "A Panic That Can Still Come Upon Me," 9.

21. Gizzi, "A Panic That Can Still Come Upon Me," 10.

22. John Keats, *Selected Letters of John Keats* (Cambridge: Harvard University Press, 2005), 291.

23. Duncan, *Truth and Life of Myth*, 13.

24. Gizzi, "A Panic That Can Still Come Upon Me," 11.

Poetic Geometries

1. Herman Melville, *Moby-Dick* (New York: Modern Library, 1952), 175.

2. Melville, *Moby-Dick*, 182.

3. Melville, *Moby-Dick*, 72.

4. Melville, *Moby-Dick*, 161.

5. Melville, *Moby-Dick*, 203.

6. Melville, *Moby-Dick*, 79.

7. Melville, *Moby-Dick*, 79.

8. Melville, *Moby-Dick*, 80.

9. Melville, *Moby-Dick*, 224.

10. Melville, *Moby-Dick*, 227.

11. Melville, *Moby-Dick*, 270.

12. Melville, *Moby-Dick*, 414–15.

13. Melville, *Moby-Dick*, 386.

14. Melville, *Moby-Dick*, 448–49.

15. Melville, *Moby-Dick*, 195.

16. Melville, *Moby-Dick*, 196.

17. Melville, *Moby-Dick*, 269–70.

18. John Keats, *Selected Letters of John Keats*, ed. Grant F. Scott (Cambridge, MA: Belknap Press, 2002),__.

19. Melville, *Moby-Dick*, 158.

20. Melville, *Moby-Dick*, 160.

21. Melville, *Moby-Dick*, 161–62.

What Kind of Monster Am I?

1. Plato, *Selected Dialogues of Plato: The Benjamin Jowett Translation*, trans. Benjamin Jowett (New York: Modern Library, 2000), 118.

2. Anne Carson, *Eros the Bittersweet* (Champaign, IL: Dalkey Archive Press, 1998), 53.

3. Carson, *Eros the Bittersweet*, 70.

4. Carson, *Eros the Bittersweet*, 75.

5. Carson, *Eros the Bittersweet*, 39.

6. Carson, *Eros the Bittersweet*, 109.

7. Carson, *Eros the Bittersweet*, 152–53.

Ghosting the Line

1. Susan Howe, "Silence Wager Stories," *The Nonconformist's Memorial* (New York: New Directions, 1993), 56–57.

2. Susan Howe, *Souls of the Labadie Tract* (New York: New Directions, 2007), 15.

3. Herman Melville, "The Lee Shore," in *Moby-Dick* (Oxford: Oxford University Press, 2008), 94.

4. Howe, "Silence Wager Stories," *Nonconformist's Memorial*, 36.

5. Susan Howe, *Singularities* (Middletown, CT: Wesleyan University Press, 1990), 50.

6. Howe, *Singularities*, 49.

7. Howe, *Nonconformist's Memorial*, 74.

8. Henry David Thoreau, "Feb. 9, 1841," *The Journal of Henry David Thoreau*, Vol. 1: *1837-1855* (New York: Dover Books, 1962), 71.

9. Howe, "Silence Wager Stories," *Nonconformist's Memorial*, 38.

10. Giorgio Agamben, "Philosophical Archaeology," in *The Signature of All Things: On Method*, trans. Luca di Santo, et al. (New York: Zone Books, 2009), 95.

11. Howe, *Nonconformist's Memorial*, 69, 16.

12. Howe, *Nonconformist's Memorial*, 26.

13. Howe, *Nonconformist's Memorial*, 75.

14. Howe, *Singularities*, 30.

15. Giorgio Agamben, "Chapter 13: *Spiriticus phantasticus*," in *Stanzas: Word and Phantasm in Western Culture*, trans. Robert L. Martinez (Minneapolis: University of Minneapolis Press, 1992), 94.

16. Howe, *Nonconformist's Memorial*, 42.

17. Howe, *Singularities*, 40.

18. Howe, *Singularities*, 43.

19. Howe, *Nonconformist's Memorial*, 61.

20. Howe, *Souls of the Labadie Tract*, 120.

21. Howe, *Souls of the Labadie Tract*, 122.

22. William Wordsworth and Samuel Taylor Coleridge, Preface to the *Lyrical Ballads*, in *Lyrical Ballads* (Oxford: Oxford University Press, 2013), 104.

23. Howe, *Singularities*, 41.

24. Agamben, *Signature of All Things: On Method.*

25. Howe, *Singularities*, 55.

26. Howe, *Souls of the Labadie Tract*, 50.

27. Howe, *Souls of the Labadie Tract*, 58.

28. Howe, *Souls of the Labadie Tract*, 55.

29. Howe, *Nonconformist's Memorial*, 39.

30. Howe, *Nonconformist's Memorial*, 34.

31. Gerald Bruns, "The Concepts of Art and Poetry in Emmanuel Levinas's Writings," in *The Cambridge Companion to Levinas*, eds. Simon Critchley and Robert Beresoni (Cambridge: Cambridge University Press, 2002), 206–234.

32. Susan Howe, *That This* (New York: New Directions, 2010), 104.

Thinking as Burial Practice

1. Henry David Thoreau, *Walden* (Boston: Beacon Press, 2004), 92.

2. Thoreau, *Walden*, 85.

3. Thoreau, *Walden*, 84.

4. Ralph Waldo Emerson, "The Poet," in *The Essential Writings of Ralph Waldo Emerson*, ed. Brooks Anderson (New York: Modern Library, 2000), 294.

5. Emerson, "The Poet," 296.

6. Ludwig Wittgenstein, *Tractatus Logico-Philosophicus*, trans. C. K. Ogden (Mineola, NY: Dover Publications, 1998), 106.

7. Emily Dickinson, "640," in *The Complete Poetry of Emily Dickinson*, ed. Thomas H. Johnson (New York: Little, Brown, 1961), 317.

8. Dickinson, *Complete Poetry of Emily Dickinson*, 128–29.

"The Oracular Tree Acquiring"

1. Henry David Thoreau, in *Poems for the Millennium*, vol. 3, ed. Jerome Rothenberg et al. (Berkeley: University of California Press, 2009), 723–724.

2. John Keats, in *Poems for the Millennium*, vol. 3, 308–311.

3. Ralph Waldo Emerson, *Emerson's Essays* (New York: Harper & Row, 1926), 276.

4. Samuel Taylor Coleridge, *Biographia Literaria* (Aukland, NZ: Floating Press, 2009), 276.

5. William Blake, in *Poems for the Millennium*, vol. 3, 95.

6. William Wordsworth, in *Poems for the Millennium*, vol. 3, 160–81.

7. Ralph Waldo Emerson, in *Poems for the Millennium*, vol. 3, 907–908.

8. Percy Bysshe Shelley, "Defence," in *Poems for the Millennium*, vol. 3, 902–903.

9. Keats, in *Poems for the Millennium*, vol. 3, 904–905.

10. Wordsworth, in *Poems for the Millennium*, vol. 3, 898.

Epistemic Flow

1. Samuel Taylor Coleridge, "Kubla Khan," *Poems and Prose* (New York: Alfred A. Knopf, 1997), 11.

2. Plato, *Cratylus*, trans. Harold North Fowler (Cambridge, MA: Loeb Classical Library, vol. 167 (Cambridge, MA: Harvard University Press, 1926), 99.

3. Jorge Luis Borges, "Pierre Menard, Author of the *Quixote*," *Labyrinths*, ed. Donald A. Yates and James E. Irby (New York: New Directions, 2007), 38.

4. John Keats, *Selected Letters of John Keats*, ed. Grant F. Scott (Cambridge, MA: Harvard University Press, 2002), 195.

Lyric Consciousness

1. Plato, *Theaetetus, Sophist*, trans. Harold North Fowler (Cambridge, MA: Loeb Classical Library, 1921), 55.

2. Exodus 20:4, King James Version.

3. Emily Dickinson, *849*, ed. R. W. Franklin (Cambridge, MA: Belknap Press, 1998), 798.

4. Dickinson, *849*, 798.

5. Dickinson, *849*, 798–99.

6. Dickinson, *849*, 799.

7. Martin Heidegger, "What Calls for Thinking?," *Basic Writings*, ed. David Farrell Krell (San Francisco: HarperSanFrancisco, 1977), 370.

8. Heidegger, "What Calls for Thinking?", 369.

9. Heidegger, "What Calls for Thinking?", 372.

10. Heidegger, "What Calls for Thinking?", 374.

11. Robert Duncan, "Often I am permitted to return to a meadow," *Selected Poems*, ed. Robert J. Bertholf (New York: New Directions, 1997), 54.

12. Heidegger, "What Calls for Thinking?", 388.

13. Heidegger, "What Calls for Thinking?", 379.

14. Plato, *Theaetetus, Sophist*, trans. Harold North Fowler, 215.

The Road Up Is the Road Down

1. Lewis Hyde, *Trickster Makes This World: Mischief, Myth, and Art* (New York: Farrar, Straus and Giroux, 2010), 318.

2. Translation mine.

3. Translation mine.

4. Translation mine.

5. Translation mine.

6. Martin Heidegger, *Being & Time*, trans. Joan Stambaugh (Albany: SUNY Press, 2010), 69.

7. Ovid, *The Metamorphoses*, trans. Allen Mandelbaum (New York: Harcourt Brace, 1993), 325.

8. Maurice Blanchot, *The Space of Literature*, trans. Ann Smock (Lincoln: University of Nebraska Press), 173.

9. Elizabeth Sewell, *The Orphic Voice* (New York: New York Review of Books Press, 2022), 1.

10. Maurice Blanchot, *The Space of Literature*, 172.

11. Translation mine.

12. Translation mine.

Circularities

1. John Keats, "This Living Hand," *Complete Poems*, ed. Jack Stillinger (Cambridge, MA: Belknap Press, 1991), 384.

2. Wallace Stevens, "Anecdote of the Jar," *The Collected Poems of Wallace Stevens*, ed. Chris Byers (New York: Vintage, 1991), 81.